ADJUSTING TO LIFE'S CHANGING SEASONS

Leon D. Pamphile

Hamilton Books
A member of
The Rowman & Littlefield Publishing Group
Lanham · Boulder · New York · Toronto · Plymouth, UK

Copyright © 2013 by
Hamilton Books
4501 Forbes Boulevard
Suite 200
Lanham, Maryland 20706
Hamilton Books Acquisitions Department (301) 459-3366

10 Thornbury Road
Plymouth PL6 7PP
United Kingdom

All rights reserved

British Library Cataloging in Publication Information Available

Library of Congress Control Number: 2013933683
ISBN: 978-0-7618-6107-2

DEDICATION

This book is gratefully dedicated to Carolyn Spicer Russ, for her big generous heart and for superbly enhancing my scholarship.

It is not the strongest of the species that survives, or the most intelligent, but the one most responsive to change.

—Charles Darwin

Contents

Prologue	ix
Acknowledgments	xiii

Part One:
EMPOWERED FOR A CHANGING SELF

1. The Path to Spiritual Empowerment	3
2. The Power to Monitor	13
3. The Power to Adjust	21

Part Two:
EMPOWERED FOR A CHANGING WORLD

4. Grace for All Seasons	31
5. Anchor for a Changing World	41
6. Managing the Stress of Time	49

Part Three:
EMPOWERED AS A CHANGE AGENT

7. Managing Your Health in a Changing World	59
8. Managing the Stress of Relational Life	67
9. Embracing Change	77
Epilogue	85
Bibliography	87

Prologue

June 24, 2008, is to me the epitome of the unexpected. Early morning that day, a dozen members of the medical mission team that came with me to Haiti from the United States boarded our rented gray van to travel to the Thomassin mountains for our last clinic day. Felix, our easygoing and reliable driver, navigated the ten miles of the uphill and curvy roads from Petion-Ville to our appointed destination with amazing ease. When we arrived, I was surprised to see a very large crowd patiently waiting to be seen.

Our doctors, nurses, and other volunteers immediately began setting up the rooms and the improvised pharmacy for our patients. Each of us was focused on the task of caring. This mixed crowd of both young and old traveled from afar to seek relief from the many ailments that troubled their lives.

The routine of caring for patients was interrupted when I saw two men struggling to carry a disabled patient to us. I recognized the man. He was Amos, my 34-year-old nephew. Two physicians and a nurse were quickly alerted to this emergency and put Amos on the cement floor. Amos was struggling to breathe. His heart had stopped. A nurse administered CPR in a desperate move to save his life. Everyone soon realized their efforts were fruitless. One of them said the painfully obvious fact: The patient was not responding. There was no escaping the dark reality that was overtaking our universe. This young man had died. With a sorrowful sigh, they did what they had to do: shift their attention to the more than one hundred living souls that still needed their care.

I came to this mountainous area that summer wanting to nurture good health and promote life. For the first time in my life I witnessed the common experience of transition from life to death. Sooner or later everyone will die. But I had never seen anyone at the moment of death.

The death of my nephew Amos showed me how quickly and radically change invades our lives. Change occurs without an alarm. Change also brings with it stress not just for me but also for my family. In this case, Amos' death came as a major life event and one of the most stressful situations I have ever encountered. I had to rise to the occasion and adjust to the new reality of life without my nephew.

Amos was the only child of my younger sister Eunide. On so many occasions, I have counseled others to monitor and adjust when faced with unexpected turmoil. Never before had I been challenged so strongly to muster the strength to help our family through this unfortunate crisis. I needed to find the wisdom and sensitivity to break the news to my sister, to Amos' wife, and especially to my almost ninety-one-year-old father whose own fragile life, would be severely affected by Amos' untimely death. I summed up my strength to rise up and prayed for help.

Change is one of the passwords we use to describe the moving reality of our lives. We wish to live with the highest sense of stability over our world and daily environment. It is not a new idea. Throughout time we have sought equilibrium in our lives. Past generations thought our universe could offer this comfort. During the late eighteenth and early nineteenth centuries, evolving scientific theories comforted our forefathers with such a sense of security. They believed they were living in a stable universe. English scientist Sir Isaac Newton proposed his theories of a universal order. According to his scientific world view, the planets were stable and self-regulating.

Yet beyond this seeming regularity, later theories show our world is full of surprises. Charles Darwin, who redefined biological science, described his unprecedented concept of evolution. We learn from him that life is not so static. "Today, in spite of the web of law, that network of forces which the past century sought to string to the ends of the universe, a strange unexpectedness lingers about our world."[1] There will be future events that escape our control altogether.

Forays across our world already suggest that "man's dream of mastering all aspects of nature takes no account of his limitations in time and space or his own senses, augmented though they may be by technical devices."[2]

The sudden death of my nephew brought with it a ripple effect. A number of changes and issues suddenly needed our immediate attention. First, I had to start thinking about burial. All my personal plans needed to change. I had planned to return to the United States on Saturday. This, too, was no longer possible.

Since change impacts our daily lives in such a profound and drastic way, it is good to be well-armed to manage its impact on us. We have a great need to be mentally and spiritually conditioned with the relevant attitude to monitor and adjust to the events and circumstances that unwittingly come our way.

Jesus offers us the help we need to work out the transition conducive to maintain our own balance and stability. Journeying with him offers the wonder-working power to manage the unexpected and inevitable changes we must encounter at every contour and detour of life's journey.

This book seeks to help you manage the challenges in an ever-changing world. It will help you secure the power to monitor and to adjust to the changes taking place in your very life, both from within or without. Finally, it motivates you to rise above these "changes" to manage your well-being and to do things for the benefit of humanity. For we believe that God destines us to become stewards of a better world while endowed with the gift of life.

My journey with the expression *monitor and adjust* began in the mid-eighties as an educator with the Pittsburgh Public Schools. It was one of the many instructional tools used for effective teaching. It was also a ready-made strategy to handle unexpected situations invading the classroom. This expression is also relevant to the countless everyday situations we face.

By *monitoring*, I mean the use of our cognitive faculties. The French philosopher René Descartes asserts that we are thinking beings in his statement "Cogito, ergo sum" (I think, therefore I am). God's word also challenges us to make greater and better use of our minds. Jesus warns to use your cognitive faculties to avoid all forms of deceptions and pitfalls. In the same way, the authors of wisdom literature bid us to carefully think before we speak and to think before we act. They remind us that "the wisdom of the prudent is to give thought to their ways."[3]

Monitoring brings an awareness of our current reality. It forces us to assess our present situation and prepare for possible changes. As a result, we are in a position to make the necessary adjustment. By monitoring and adjusting to the fluidity of life situations, we can have a more effective spiritual management of our lives.

These chapters describe various strategies to help you develop and maintain some effective principles of life. They seek to propel you to a position of strength so as to make the best of the changes that affect us daily. We write with the unshakable confidence that God helps build an inner strength to handle the stress of change. He stands ready to help you live an abundant life he has designed just for you as individual in his vast universe.

NOTES

1. Loren Eiseley, The Unexpected Universe (San Diego: A Harvest/HBJ Book, 1969), 41.
2. Ibid., 42.
3. Proverbs 14:8.

Acknowledgments

I am deeply indebted to several people in the writing of this book over the last six years. I am always thankful to Rozelle, my dear wife, for supporting me in everything I do by her encouragement and the freedom she gives me to carry out my many activities. I am grateful to Thomas Forgrave for reading this work with utmost care and his words of encouragement. Carolyn Russ, who gracefully accepted to read the text in spite of her professional commitments, made invaluable suggestions. Joseph Plummer, my final reviewer, formatted the text for publication. May the Lord bless and reward each one of you in every way for your kindness.

Part One

EMPOWERED FOR A CHANGING SELF

Chapter One

The Path to Spiritual Empowerment

> I have told you these things, so that in me you may have peace. In this world you will have trouble. But take heart! I have overcome the world. (John 16:33)

Gideon came from the tribe of Manasseh. In the history of Israel, he stands as a remarkable example of an individual known for his extraordinary service. Gideon made a tremendous contribution to his people at a time when Israel was losing control of her land to neighboring tribes (the Midianites and Amalekites). These tribes spread terror throughout Israel by their frequent pillages. At this very time, an angel of the Lord appeared to Gideon while he was tending to his wheat. The angel challenged him to become the one to deliverer Israel from these invaders. At first Gideon looked at his liabilities, and shied away. Yet these liabilities became assets when he made the decision to embrace this call to action. As we look at this incident and the subsequent extraordinary changes that took place in Gideon's life, we are encouraged to follow his example.

Gideon's experience offers us important clues on our own path to understanding. It shows us that true empowerment comes from God. It begins with the consciousness of being in God's presence. The process moves forward with our willingness to be clothed with divine power. It reaches then the climactic stage of conducting our lives in the parameter of the will of God. The interrelated combination of God's presence, power, and will works to construct an unmovable spiritual foundation for the individual in tune with God's universal purpose.

THE SCOPE OF EMPOWERMENT

Empowerment helps individuals and groups take steps to overcome their own weaknesses and disabilities. The *Oxford American Desk Dictionary* defines the word "empower" as to "authorize" and to "make able." It has become a buzzword with the legal meaning to "invest with power." It relates to the practice of permitting legal representatives to complete certain specific tasks when the person cannot be there. It can also be the power of attorney given on behalf of a cognitively impaired individual.

Empowerment also conveys the idea "to supply with an ability, to enable." The ideology of empowerment was evident in politics as a password widely used in the civil rights movement and the women's rights movement. Nanette Page in her article "Empowerment: What Is It?" highlights the concept as "a multi-dimensional process that helps people to gain control over their own lives."[1] She asserts that at the core of its meaning lies the idea of power. When people acquire power, they will use it for their own lives, their communities, and their society.

Education is the best example of a tool helping the individual through a virtual transformation in countless ways. Any look at the trajectory of President Obama's political career reveals how education helped him reach his current position. His training at both Columbia and Harvard gave him the foundation to aspire to great things.

Empowerment is a multidimensional concept, but here, we focus on the spiritual dimension of power rooted in God. In His wisdom is found the staying power that allows us to monitor and adjust effectively to life's seasons of change and the countless forms and shapes connected with the stress of change.

IN GOD'S PRESENCE

Gideon's original response was to refuse to listen to the angel's call. He was certainly not going to go off to the battlefield for Israel. His reluctance was like that of Moses and other prophets who received similar calls. "How can I save Israel? My clan is the weakest in Manasseh and I am the least in my family."[2] No doubt Gideon was also plagued by the stress of uncertainty as he looked at his choices.

That attitude was positively altered when Gideon realized he was not going alone in a venture that would test his abilities. The Lord promised to be with him. This promise gave him the courage needed by all those who dare make the commitment of becoming an instrument of change for God and for humanity.

God's presence also gives us comfort to manage life's stresses. Our relationship with Christ positions us for victorious living. I was able to successfully manage the change triggered by my nephew's death because I knew the Lord stood with me.

SPIRITUALLY FIGHTING-FIT

In Greek history, there were the two important city states of Sparta and Athens. When the Spartans arrived, they enslaved the inhabitants. As a result, they realized they had to be strong to defend their freedom at any moment. Spartans came then to have one aim in life: "to be fighting fit." To that end their young were trained to endure hardships, hunger, and cold and to deny pleasures.

Just like the Spartans, we need to train ourselves to become and to remain spiritually fighting fit. When our spirit reaches that level, we gain the confidence of "being strengthened with all power according to his glorious might so that you may have great endurance and patience, and joyfully giving thanks to the Father."[3]

Power here means both endurance and patience. The Scottish theologian William Barclay describes endurance as our ability to handle circumstances, while patience allows us to deal effectively with people. No one can successfully handle the ongoing stress of changes in life without both endurance and patience. Together, these two virtues help us to becoming "fighting fit."

EMPOWERED THROUGH CHRIST

Consider this: Jesus launched his ministry by enrolling a number of men he met through a series of encounters. While walking by the Sea of Galilee, he met Andrew and his brother Simon as they were casting nets into the lake. He signed them up in the new volunteer army of his new kingdom of justice and righteousness. Their lives were changed forever as Christ transformed them into "fishers of men."

Other lives were also bettered because of their encounter with Jesus. Bartimaeus conquered his blindness. When he became aware Jesus was passing, he rose to follow him, calling out, "Jesus, Son of David, have mercy on me."[4] When Jesus saw his faith, he immediately healed Bartimaeus, restoring his sight. He was cured not only of a horrible physical illness but also an equally debilitating spiritual blindness. He received a brand new vision to chart a new course for his life.

Bartimaeus teaches us the need to monitor, to be aware of a possible encounter with the divine. It should be the desire of everyone who strives to improve their life. To enhance our position or situation, we often covet meetings and interviews with the rich and famous. A friend of mine recently sent me a picture showing her beaming smile with former President George W. Bush. An encounter with God is always transformational. We reap invaluable dividends by living in the presence of God.

Let's call these two examples serendipitous. They happened without any premeditated intervention. Here's another inspiring case as we look at Zacchaeus' deliberate effort to seek an encounter with Jesus. I would call this kind of determination a "purposeful encounter." Zacchaeus was the infamous tax collector known for his unusually small stature. By monitoring his environment, he noticed the crowd jostling around Jesus. Zacchaeus ran ahead of the throng and climbed a sycamore-fig tree to better see Jesus. His determination paid off handsomely, for beyond his wildest expectation, Jesus called to him. Bypassing the well-to-do and respected citizens of Jericho, Jesus chose to spend a day at the house of Zacchaeus.

Zacchaeus was a problem solver who filled his hunger for God and was able to transcend a less-than-flattering past when he met Jesus. The potential for change is exponential when the right connection takes place. Christ is the supreme friend who empowers men and women to monitor and adjust their situation to their benefit.

God's presence displays a conquering mindset with all of life's stressful changes. God's presence ushers in an aura of brightness and radiance. For instance, his presence shining through the burning bush caught Moses' attention and turned his life in a new direction. Moses left his comfort zone in Pharaoh's palace, choosing to "be mistreated with the people of God rather to enjoy the pleasures of sin for a short time."[5]

IN GOD'S POWER

An encounter with Christ lets people monitor their lives to adjust to the stress of change. It is essentially a way of coping with the changes that will inevitably come and learn to make the relevant adjustments to reduce the stress. Divine power provides both the authority and the ability.

EMPOWERED WITH AUTHORITY

Jesus sent out a group of men to be fishers of men. They had neither secular nor religious training. Peter and his brother Andrew were fishermen. Matthew was a tax collector. Christ gave them a new mission and the power to fulfill that mission. He gave them the authority to combat evil forces, drive out the demons, and heal the sick. They also had the power to confidently face an uncertain future. That power meant putting one's life on the line.

Peter and John used their power to heal a crippled beggar at the temple gate called Beautiful. This healing upset the religious hierarchy, who saw this miraculous healing as a threat to their own authority. The religious leaders brought Peter and John before the Sanhedrin, the religious court, to explain their actions.

Undoubtedly this trial was a life-threatening event for these two disciples. Yet during the proceedings, the pair had a courage that amazed their accusers, who came to the conclusion that nothing could possibly explain the boldness of these unschooled and ordinary men except the fact that they "had been with Jesus,"[6] who they also considered a rebel.

EMPOWERED WITH ABILITY

Christ's empowerment extends beyond his few disciples to all those who seek him. He gives the ability to overcome the forces that interfere with our divine potential. Augustine found the power in Christ to change his life. He had a troubled youth bent on rebellion and pleasures. Though his mother Monica tried to bring him up as a Christian, he was rather pulled to the worldly attraction of sex, fame, and power. At the age of eighteen, Augustine had a mistress who gave him a son.

Augustine's mother was not the least bit satisfied with this lifestyle, and, he admitted to himself, neither was he. He sought to conquer these fleshly passions. It was not so until he was walking in a garden one afternoon. He heard what seemed to be a child's voice saying over and over, "Take up and read." He found a collection of Paul's epistles that happened to be on a nearby table and opened it to read. The first thing he saw was this passage: "Not in reveling and drunkenness, not in lust and wantonness, not in quarrels and rivalries. Rather arm yourselves with the Lord Jesus Christ, spend no more thought on nature and nature's appetites."[7]

That was all it took. From that moment, Augustine found the divine power to change his life. Following his conversion, he left Rome to return to Hippo in North Africa where he was later ordained a priest and consecrated as the bishop of Hippo. He became the intellectual architect of the Middle-Ages and one of the greatest theologians of worldwide Christianity.

EMPOWERED WITH SELF-CONTROL

Dominique Strauss-Kahn is a French economist, lawyer, and member of the French Socialist Party who, for four years, served as the managing director of the International Monetary Fund (IMF). All eyes were on him to become the next president of France in the 2012 election. All the honor, power, and hope invested in him were wiped out when he reportedly assaulted a 32-year-old maid in the Sofitel New York Hotel. Though Strauss-Kahn was cleared of any charges because the victim lacked credibility, he later acknowledged his moral failure.

Self is our greatest enemy. We are engaged in an inner struggle between the flesh and the Spirit. It is a struggle manifested through the passions, addictions, and various demons that make up the human personality. Failure to conquer these demons has led many people to self-defeat and self-destruction. God gives us spiritual power to monitor the self and adjust to the timeless principles we want to achieve. It is important we use this self-control as power for our own fulfillment.

The American statesman William Jennings Bryan said, "Destiny is not a matter of chance; it is a matter of choice." God's power helps us shape our destiny. It is sad to see those people who waste their potential just because they lack the power to conquer their addictions, their slothfulness, and their confusion. It takes staying power to use our creativity and determination to achieve purpose.

TRANSFORMING POWER

Martin Luther King, Jr., carried out his God-given mission. He became America's most significant civil rights leader. In the course of mass protests against racial injustices, his words and deeds inspired millions throughout the world. In 1964, he won the Nobel Peace Prize for his leadership. He was able to attain this honor because he leaned on divine power to conquer the mounting stress of the threats to his life.

Throughout the Montgomery bus boycott, he was subjected to incredible pressure. He was arrested and thrown in jail. In 1956, he received a midnight hate call that made him fear for his family's safety. In those dark hours, he was able to go on because, as he explains, "At that moment I experienced the presence of the divine as I had never experienced him before. It seemed as though I could hear the quiet assurance of an inner voice saying, 'Stand up for righteousness, stand up for truth; and God will be at your side forever.'"[8] God's power strengthens us to face courageously the unknown and to bear the unbearable.

IN GOD'S WILL

I was born and raised in the Haitian countryside. During my first twelve years, I enjoyed wholehearted communion with nature. I was comfortable wandering the lush courtyard of my father's and grandfather's estate. To this day, I still recall at sunset the harmonious concert orchestrated by the birds and insects filling our surroundings.

In this unforgettably peaceful setting, I climbed the trees both small and large. Once, though, I lost my balance as I hoisted my body up the branches of a mango tree beside the house, and fell. I don't quite remember what happened except I lost my balance and fell to the ground like a dead weight. Fortunately, I was spared from any serious injury.

Many years later I realized my fall was connected to my unknowing violation of the law of gravity. Its discovery is recalled in a well-known little legend when Sir Isaac Newton sat under an apple tree and an apple fell on his head. This benign incident led him to the insight of the gravitational force pulling the apple down to the earth. The law of universal gravitation was discovered as a force to reckon with in the evolution of science. Had I known of Newton's law of gravitational force, I might have thought twice about climbing that mango tree.

Awareness of gravitation helps us understand the need to abide by God's will. Just as it is impossible to ignore gravity when handling nature, it is also necessary to keep ourselves in tune with God's will as a force of monitoring and adjusting to life's changing situations. Obedience to God's will yields unbelievable spiritual power to handle both the ponderable and the imponderable situations facing us. It is also a powerful way to reduce the stress that can adversely affect our health.

BEWARE OF GOING AGAINST GOD'S WILL

Going against God's will is like sailing into contrary winds. The startling story of Balaam illustrates the foolishness of such a course of action. Balaam was a master soothsayer of his generation. He also had the power to put a curse on others. He was asked by King Belak of Moab to place a curse on the Israelites so he could defeat them. King Balak resorted to this drastic action to protect his kingdom once he learned how the Israelites had already defeated the Amorites. Balak's will was, however, on a collision course with God's will. No need to guess whose will would ultimately triumph.

Though Balak promised to reward Balaam most handsomely with silver and gold, the plot would fail. Balak led the soothsayer to three different sites to speak his curse. Each time, Balaam instead spoke a doxology expressing thoughts favorable to Israel. "How can I curse those whom God has not cursed? How can I denounce those whom God has not denounced?"[8] A frustrated Balak had no choice but to accept the fact that he could not overrule what God had ordained by either money or military power.

THE BLESSINGS OF DOING GOD'S WILL

Since human will is subject to God's will, we truly find power to monitor and adjust to life's situations when we are assured we are acting using God's will. Joseph found the power to perform superbly as prime minister in Egypt because he realized he was performing his duties within the parameter of God's will. As the story goes, the Pharaoh had a couple of dreams that left him utterly disturbed. On the suggestion of his butler, he asked Joseph to interpret his dreams. Joseph helped him understand the dreams were a revelation of God's purpose for his nation. As Joseph told the king, "The matter has been firmly decided by God, and He will do it soon."[9]

Joseph asks the Pharaoh to accept God's will by taking the necessary steps to cope with the prediction of the upcoming time of abundance and famine. It was a matter of using wisdom to make the best of the situation. The Pharaoh rewarded Joseph as the "discerning and wise man" to take charge. He invested him with the power to develop and implement the necessary plan to get the nation ready for this critical time. Joseph was able to complete this function with great distinction because he knew that he had the will of God on his side.

The conviction of doing God's will drives away the feelings of frustration and fear we have when dealing with uncertainty and doubt. I often get lost when I go to places I do not know. Anyone who identifies with me knows the pain and frustration involved in getting lost. To operate in the will of God is like being guided by a GPS that eliminates the stress connected with the uncertainty of our destination. Knowledge in this case is power. We have the conviction we are moving in the right direction.

No one in his right mind ever tries to go into battle without being properly armed. Such an action would be a self-destructing move. Proper equipment is necessary to assure ultimate victory. It is also unwise to pretend being on the battlefield of life without strength. Our empowerment stems from being always in God's presence, God's power, and God's will. This is the path to invincibility as we face life's adversities.

NOTES

1. Nanette Page, "Empowerment: What Is It?", *Journal of Extension*, October 1999, http/www.joe.org/joe/1999Octobercomml/pt, access date 2/11/2013
2. Judges 6:15.

3. Colossians 1:11.
4. Mark 11:47.
5. Hebrews 11:25.
6. Acts 4:13.
7. Romans 13:13-14.
8. Numbers 23:8.
9. Genesis 41:32.

Chapter Two

The Power to Monitor

> Be very careful, then, how you live—not as unwise, but as wise.[1] (Ephesians 5:15)

Aesop teaches the importance of monitoring life's every situation. He shares some insight in his story of the frogs and the well. Two frogs lived together in a marsh. One hot summer the marsh dried up, so they left for another place. In time, they came to a well, and one of them looked into it and said to the other: "This looks a nice cool place. Let us jump in and settle there." But the other, who was much wiser, replied: "Not so fast, my friend. Supposing this well dried up like the marsh, how should we get out again?"

The lesson of the frogs is that we need to think twice before acting. Making effective use of our minds is the cornerstone of monitoring.

MONITORING OUR ENVIRONMENT

The *Dictionary of Psychology* defines the verb "to monitor" as a mental exercise where the goal is to "observe carefully with the intention to diagnose or evaluate what is happening and to be ready to interfere in the growing process if considered necessary."[2] We are divinely equipped with the cognitive skills of reason, attention, and intelligence to monitor life's changes. In defining intelligence in their book *Psychology: An Introduction*, Kagan and Havemann describe the role it plays in this monitoring exercise. They say intelligence is the "ability to profit from experience, learn new information, and adjust to new situations."[3] When we put this ability to work, it helps us to assess our circumstances to make the most informed decisions.

Applied cognitive psychology highlights the use of the mind to monitor complex mechanical systems. Traffic controllers and those who monitor life support systems are examples of individuals with high-stress jobs. The level of attention required by these tasks is tremendous. When we don't devote the required attention to a particular task, we perform below our effectiveness level.

Aesop's story of the two frogs helps to motivate us to devote this higher level of attention in any decision-making process. It features two kinds of frogs in our world: the wise and the wiser one. Both faced a vital issue connected with their physical environment. The wiser one managed to avoid the pitfalls of the well. We should imitate him as we seek to monitor and adjust to our daily physical and psychological challenges.

Our cognitive skills must reinforce our spiritual power. We pity those who rely solely on their brain power and neglect the tested wisdom of God's word to monitor the stress of change and make adjustments. We are reminded how a solid spiritual foundation enhances our thoughts and behavior. In the end, only God allows us to see our shortcomings and take corrective actions. He will set us on a viable path to manage the changes in our lives.

NOAH'S MONITORING APPROACH

Consider Noah's experience as an example of the monitoring process. His story is marked by the monumental changes that took place in both the world of his time and Noah's life due to the flood. Noah took monitoring steps before and after this catastrophe.

As a man who walked with God, Noah had divine guidance and "did everything just as God commanded him."[4] With a deep sense of responsibility, he faithfully followed the script God had drafted for him. Forewarned is forearmed, according to the maxim. He built an ark on God's instructions that made it possible for him and his family to survive the forty days and forty nights of torrential rains.

After the flood, Noah eventually then wondered how he would get off the ark. He had a strategy that unfolded in a step-by-step approach. First, he sent out a raven. It flew back and forth until the earth was dry. Later, he sent out a dove. It came back because it could not find a place to land. Seven days later, he again released the dove. This time it returned with an olive leaf in its beak. It was this first sign of hope that kept Noah going. He waited another seven days before releasing the dove again. Now, he had proof the waters had dried enough since the dove did not return. Noah's monitoring power illustrates patience at its highest level. It took Noah another twenty-nine days before he finally made his way out of the ark.

When we walk with God, it is possible to find the intelligence and wisdom to monitor the flood-like situations of life. We live in a world subject to an ever-quickening degree of change. The monitoring skill helps us survive. It must apply to all areas of our lives including what we eat, what we drink, and what we breathe. We must pay attention to all forms of physical and even moral pollution.

PAUL'S MONITORING APPROACH

The Apostle Paul went to Jerusalem to bring much needed financial help for the poor. Though he brought aid, things turned upside down when he was arrested during a visit to the temple on the trumped up charge of teaching against the Jewish law. The case was heard before the Sanhedrin, the Jewish religious court, before civil, if not military, courts involving such high Roman figures as the governors Festus and Felix and the king Agrippa. Paul was not at all satisfied with these deliberations and asked to appeal his case to Caesar. Because of this appeal, he got to make the improbable journey to Rome, where he experienced the most unpredictable development.

When all arrangements were finally made, Paul boarded the ship along with fellow prisoners for what was a journey into the unknown. The sailors took their jobs seriously and kept to a definite schedule. Quickly, it became necessary to monitor and adjust to the changes from the unpredictable weather that came their way. Or, as King Solomon said, "Many are the plans in a man's heart, but it is the Lord's purpose that prevails."[5]

The mariners were to sail along the Turkish coast, but soon heavy winds forced them into their first deviation. Head winds drove them north of Cyprus into Myra.

This required a second deviation. To escape the winds, they sailed to Fair Havens where they found fair winds and remained for several days.

Despite Paul's advice to stay in port, the sailors decided to set sail. It didn't take long; the Northeaster grew into a potential catastrophe. Things on board seemed hopeless. It is a blessing that man's misfortunes always become God's opportunity. With God's help, Paul was able to give the men hope. "I urge you to keep up your courage," he told them, "because not one of you will be lost."[6]

Transformed by the sense of hope Paul gave them, the mariners steadied the ship. Again we see a progressive operation. At first, the mariners discovered the water was deep, one hundred and twenty feet deep, in fact. A second "sounding" revealed to them the depth had decreased to ninety feet. At this stage, they were able to drop four anchors from the stern and pray for daylight."[7] In the midst of the storm, the power of prayer helped calm them and enable them to think rationally to regain control of the situation.

MONITORING AS VIGILANCE

Applied cognitive psychology helps us understand that thought has an impact on behavior. In our complex society, changes take place quickly. To a large extent, we are able to cope with the new technological innovations because things are automatized for us. We rely heavily on the machines to work without thinking much about the process. We drive our cars and ride our bicycles without thinking of the mechanics and physics required to get things to move in the way we want. Paying attention to our daily activities, by monitoring them, helps us avoid the thousand and one pitfalls we come across.

National leaders have demonstrated the importance of vigilance. In the ancient world, they built impregnable walls that became hallmarks of national security strategies. Jericho was surrounded by its well-fortified walls. Joshua and his army had to rely on miraculous power to bring down these walls.

In human history, the Great Wall of China still defies human imagination, and is an example of these fortified walls. It was the enormous project carried out by Shih Huang-ti, an early Chinese emperor. Shih was not only one of the greatest warriors that there has ever been, he was also China's first emperor. He transformed the whole country. E. H. Gombrich in his *Little History of the World* described the Great Wall as "a massive construction, a double wall made of stone with tall towers and castellations, winding its symmetrical way over plains, through deep ravines and up steep mountain slopes as it follows the line of the frontier for all of four thousand miles.[8]"

He built this wall to protect his peoples from the wild tribes that threatened his empire. To get an idea of the size of this construction, consider these maths: a thousand miles is the distance between Miami and New York City. That is a distance covered in a nearly three-hour flight. The approximate length of the Wall of China would then be four times the distance between Miami and New York City. To monitor the security of his nation, Shih undertook this mind-boggling enterprise.

Throughout Israel's history, the need to be diligent was ever present. A wall was built around Jerusalem as an impregnable buffer to protect against enemy attacks. Somewhere on the top a watchtower was erected to detect the approach of their many enemies. Watchmen stood continually at their posts.[9]

So you can imagine Nehemiah's consternation when this "indestructible" wall was destroyed by the Babylonians. He was deeply troubled about the wall's destruction and conceived a plan to rebuild it. His efforts that mobilized the people for the work remain a model of inspiration for those interested in community development.

More recently, the American military establishment proposed a National Missile Defense plan to shield the United States from intercontinental ballistic missile attacks. With this plan, attack missiles would be intercepted near their launch point, during their flight through space, and during their atmospheric descent. The feasibility of such a system remains a point of debate among defense officials. Yet the timeless idea of vigilance as a subject of national security remains relevant.

INDIVIDUAL VIGILANCE

This vigilance of our national security leaders helps us understand the need for our personal vigilance. It should become obvious that we should maintain our own well-being and security. We should develop strategies to monitor our behavior to avoid hurting ourselves.

We have a good head start when it comes to our response to physical agents that threaten our survival. We have an autonomic nervous system that protects us (monitors) against danger. When our forbears faced saber-tooth tigers in the forests, their bodies reacted with both fight and a flight response. They exhibited both a physical and psychological response. At the physical level, the adrenaline activated their muscles to help them flee the danger.

An active response is also triggered at the psychological level. The mind immediately becomes mobilized for action. Our eyesight sharpens and our impulses quicken. We gain the courage to rise up to what might seem an insurmountable obstacle. Harriet Beecher Stowe provides us with a vivid illustration of the fight and flight response in her story *Uncle Tom's Cabin*. The heroic figure Eliza was an enslaved African American who was threatened with being sold with her child. Eliza seemed doomed to a life of slavery, but she managed an escape with her son. It is inspiring to imagine her escaping through the woodlands on the way to freedom, crossing the Ohio River which stood before her as the River Jordan of old.

Now slave-catchers were in pursuit. As catchers were closing in, she heard them. According to her description: "I jumped right on to the ice; and how I got across, I don't know,-but first I knew, a man was helping me up the bank."[10] Undoubtedly the physical and mental forces in the fight and flight response were put to work as she escaped, just as our ancestors ran away from the tigers.

We have timeless and proven biblical principles in our ongoing vigilant effort. The Bible teaches us that the saber-tooth tigers are still chasing us in many different shapes and forms. They can bring us down one way or another if we are not vigilant.

True vigilance begins with a healthy thought process. Paul describes it in this way: "Whatever is true, whatever is noble, whatever is right, whatever is pure, whatever is lovely, whatever is admirable, whatever is lovely, if anything excellent and praiseworthy- think about such things."[11] The monitoring process begins as we look inside ourselves to first apply our knowledge to any external threat. Our internal force helps us master the inclinations that can lead to self-defeat. These inclinations include our emotions and passions.

MONITORING THE EGO

Jesus told a powerful story highlighting two distinct egos. He described two men who went to the temple to pray. The first, a Pharisee, focusing on his achievements and his many deeds, described himself as a righteous man. He set himself above the vile company of robbers, evil doers, and adulterers. The second man, a tax collector, realizing his shortcomings, begged for mercy. The prayer of the latter man was rewarded because of his humility.

It is imperative to monitor the ego that can so easily grow into an inflated dimension. The ego can evolve into egotism, or the excessive conceit, excessive preoccupation with our self-importance. The Bible clearly teaches "clothe yourselves with humility toward one another because God opposes the proud and gives grace to the humble."[12]

USE YOUR MIND

Thinking is our most effective weapon to conquer our weaknesses. Thinking and behaving are intrinsically linked. Our deeds begin with our thought process. To be effective, Peter asks us to "be self-controlled and (be) alert. Your enemy the devil prowls around like a roaring lion looking for someone to devour."[13]

Nehemiah excelled in monitoring the pitfalls of his enemies. As he was rebuilding the walls of Jerusalem, his detractors tried to trick him into joining them in a questionable meeting. By carefully monitoring the situation, Nehemiah continued to rebuild the wall. He rebuked these men with the following message: "I am carrying on a great project and I cannot go down."[14] His use of his spiritual and cognitive skills can become an example as we seek to avoid the schemes of those who strive to destroy us.

We know that the enemy is like a wolf in sheep clothing. We must always stay on our guard to avoid deception, in its various forms and consequences.

As we move in the moveable landscape of life, it is important not only to monitor our thoughts and actions but also to make the necessary adjustment and embrace coping skills necessary for our well-being. These coping skills naturally stem from the timeless proven word of God.

NOTES

1. Ephesians 5:15.
2. Raymond Corsini, *Dictionary of Psychology* (Ann Arbor, Mich.: Braun-Brumfield, 1999), 605.
3. Jerome Kegan and Ernest Havemann, *Psychology: An Introduction.* Harcourt Brace Jovanovich, Inc. 1972), 591.
4. Genesis 6:22.
5. Proverbs 19:21.
6. Acts 27:22.
7. Acts 27:27.
8. E. H. Gombrich, *A Little History of the World* (New Haven and London: Yale University Press, 1985), 81.
9. Isaiah 21:8.
10. Harriet Beecher Stowe, *Uncle Tom's Cabin* (New York: Barnes and Noble Classics, 2003), 84.
11. Philippians 4:8.
12. I Peter 5:5.
13. I Peter 5:8.
14. Nehemiah 6:3.

Chapter Three

The Power to Adjust

> Do not conform any longer to the pattern of this world, but be transformed by the renewing of your mind. (Romans 12:2)

I arrived in Pittsburgh in the early 70s, greeted on a late December day by an especially harsh snowstorm. I had heard of snow in my native Haiti, I had read about it in books, and I had heard it romanticized in songs, but I had never experienced it.

I had had a very hospitable welcome when I landed in sunny Miami. There the adjustment was naturally easy for me. When friends invited me to come to Pittsburgh to further my education, I heartily welcomed the opportunity. Acquaintances in Miami, however, warned me about the bad weather awaiting me. In anticipation of things yet unseen, I wore a couple pair of trousers to protect my legs. In addition, I bought a winter coat. Then I boarded the plane that took me to my new destination.

Behold, I was indeed welcomed by a heavy snowstorm. All my precautionary measures paid off. In the next few days, my host took me shopping to stock up on winter gear. At first, I did not want to part with my stylish Italian shoes. I still behaved as if I were in the tropics. To this day, I remember treading in the slushy stuff with these summer shoes that soon became incredibly beaten by the elements. It took me a few weeks before I realized the urgent need to adjust to my new environment if I wanted to survive the Pittsburgh winter.

ADJUSTMENT IS A MUST

In his *Dictionary of Psychology,* Raymond J. Corsini defines adjustment as the "modification of attitudes and behavior to meet the demands of life effectively, such as carrying on constructive interpersonal relations, dealing with stressful or problematic situations, handling responsibilities, fulfilling personal needs and aims, and wearing heavier clothing in colder weather."[1]

It is a must to acquire and develop skills that let us successfully perform these various functions. The adjustment process requires an appropriate level of maturity and flexibility to complete these various tasks. We are thus called to monitor and to adjust to these changes at every turn.

It takes an inner power to navigate the choppy waters associated with change. A successful adjustment does, however, bring with it both growth and personal development. In the Letter to the Hebrews, the author challenges us to work out positive changes: "We are confident of better things in your case."[2] This prophet presses us to transform our present challenges into opportunities, to rise above our present condition to find something better. Throughout this letter, we are reminded of a better hope, a better covenant, better promises, and better things that will come. We must embrace the power necessary to work our way to a higher and better level.

MALADJUSTMENT

Unfortunately, many of us get stuck in the daily routine. As a result, we sadly fail to make any progress. Our failure puts us in the difficult position of falling into what I choose to call maladjustment.

My initial reluctance to acquire appropriate winter shoes on my arrival in Pittsburgh reflects a resistance to my new environment, a certain level of maladjustment. I was not mentally ready to make the transition from a Haitian to an American lifestyle. It was an issue of environmental adjustment. Had I not made the necessary changes, subsequently wearing different shoes, I would have felt the negative consequences of my reluctance.

I am fascinated by the story of dinosaurs. These giant animals walked the earth more than 100 million years ago. It is one of history's great mysteries, how these creatures disappeared. Scientists have put forth theories ranging from a volcanic eruption to an asteroid collision as reasons for the disappearance of the dinosaurs. While no one knows for sure, the theory of climatic changes has gained strength recently. According to this theory, dinosaurs succumbed because of their failure to adapt to the evolving environmental conditions. As dramatic swings took place in the climate, the plants that were the dinosaurs' food supply became extinct. Lacking food, the dinosaurs could not prosper.

Similarly, our survival depends to a large extent on our ability to make a timely and adequate shift to the ongoing changes of our lives. Though we don't invite change, it shows up anyway. When we fail to cope, "maladjustment" becomes an uninvited guest. A whole gamut of behavioral and emotional disorders ranging from the milder discomfort of stress to neuroses and psychotic diseases will plague us. Depending on the scope of our pain and misery, some people may need to seek professional help.

It is imperative we acquire the skills necessary to enhance adequate adjustment. It is the true path to enjoying a fulfilling life while maintaining a healthy personality.

ADJUSTMENT TO PEOPLE

Well, if we are ever going to enjoy a normal life, our first and foremost challenge is to develop what I call the loving adjustment skill, the simple strategy of learning to get along with others. This is a prime survival skill, yet it is the hardest one to learn. The Roman playwright Plautus said man is a wolf to man, a description of man's inherently selfish nature. Conquering that selfishness is a huge step along the path of living in harmony with one another.

The Bible helps us develop and sharpen that great skill: "Do nothing out of selfish ambition or vain conceit, but in humility consider others better than yourselves. Each of you should look not only to your own interests, but also to the interests of others."[3] The challenge to engage one's self for the benefit of others is an aid for learning a harmonious relationship with each person. Developing harmonious relationships grows with time. Though the results are never quick, we will gradually see the rewards when we make a commitment to adjust to our fellow human beings.

CONQUER FEARS

Love conquers fears. During the sixties, Richard Lazarus wrote a book called *Personality and Adjustment* where he discussed adjusting to people. He described how humans succeeded in controlling their environment using science and technology. Lazarus confessed, however, that man "faces annihilation at the hands of his own kind through the very technical advances that help free him from the elemental struggles. So he fears other men." Fear is one of the stumbling blocks to developing healthy interpersonal relationships. This fear injects mistrust, misunderstanding, and miscommunication. It raises hostilities between people.

Fear is a negative force that pits one group against another and nations against nations. Fear can drive international relationships to war. Citing national security, policy makers spend a lot of money to alleviate their fears, neglecting essential programs in health, education, and welfare.

Ralph Waldo Emerson suggested that love should be in the mix of international relations: "The power of love as the basis of a state has never been tried." What if the love as taught by Jesus would become the guideline used in political science? Such an approach is contrary to the way most of our leaders think. Yet this love is a powerful instrument that would transform relationships at all levels. New and innovative methods should be tried to make life more tolerable and enjoyable for all of us.

RELEASE THE POWER OF LOVE

While this idea still remains a lofty ideal, we should nevertheless strive to make love an effective weapon of interpersonal relations. The Bible teaches us, "There is no fear in love. But perfect love drives out fear."[4] Love is the greatest force in the universe. When our deeds are motivated by love, we can reach out and touch others in a very positive way. There will be a reciprocity that rewards our efforts.

By being love centered, the individual will become life changing. American psychologist Og Mandigo offers his own commitment to love: "I will greet this day with love in my heart. For this is the greatest secret of success in all ventures. Muscles can split a shield and even destroy life itself but only the unseen power of love can open the hearts of man...I will make love my greatest weapon and none on who I call can defend upon its force."[5] This is an inspiring if not irresistible call to make love one's greatest weapon. It is certainly worth trying.

In sacred literature, there are a multitude of mentions of this power of love. Solomon describes his experience as a force "strong as death and its jealousy unyielding as the grave. It burns like blazing fire, like a mighty flame. Many waters cannot quench love; rivers cannot wash it away."[6] The Apostle Paul describes love as an unfailing force: "Love always protects, always trusts, always hopes, and always perseveres. Love never fails."[7]

The power of love is timeless. Love embraced as the skill of choice in interpersonal relations will work wonders in helping people to make the necessary, if not indispensable, adjustment to others with acceptance, communication, and forgiveness.

ACCEPTANCE

Acceptance is a key attribute of love. Love works best when we accept others by looking beyond looking beyond the physical appearance to focus on their inner qualities. Acceptance allows us to take the necessary steps for peaceful and harmonious relations. The call for acceptance is loudly echoed in biblical teachings. "Accept one another... just as Christ accepted you,"[8] Paul wrote. It is a sign of deep maturity to overlook the failings and failures of others to be able to enjoy their company.

At the heart of our willingness to accept others is the very art of friendship. Thomas Hughes, British reformer, jurist, and novelist says: "Blessed are they who have the gift of making friends, for it's one of God's gifts. It involves many things, but above all, the power of going out of one's self, and appreciating whatever is noble and loving in another."[9]

COPING WITH ADVERSITY

Adversity shows up in a thousand and one shapes and forms at every turn of life's journey. There is a great need of developing coping adjustment skills to a point where we are able to cope with adversity. It is a matter here of being well conditioned to handle life's difficulties.

To "monitor and adjust" suggests it takes power to realize our plans and dreams. Since we can neither control nor escape the unforeseeable events that shape our lives, we should establish a strategy to cope with life's problems. Joseph teaches us that effective coping adjustment skills can hinge on the abiding presence of God at every step. Joseph relied on God to overcome the many adverse situations he faced.

Joseph had a couple of dreams that forecast his future elevation. From the moment he shared them, his life became unsettled. His father detected a slight arrogance in Joseph. "What is this dream you had? Will your mother and I and your brother actually come and bow down to the ground before you?"[10] Joseph's brothers even tried to get rid of this dreamer by throwing him down in a well. They sold him to Ishmaelite merchants, who were trafficking in human flesh.

Through God's presence, Joseph coped with these horrific circumstances. He endured the unjust, false accusation from his master's wife that landed him in jail. In the end, he overcame all obstacles to emerge as the prime minister of Egypt. Adversity was successfully handled by his conviction of the presence of God.

Helen Keller's name is inked as one of the heroes who found how to overcome adversity. Because of her blindness and deafness, she faced tremendous challenges. Yet she discovered the indomitable determination to overcome these obstacles. As she put it, "All the world is full of suffering. It is also full of overcoming." She remains a source of inspiration to us all with her achievements. Her thrilling and fascinating life demonstrates that she was able to overcome a most profound adversity.

In these two characters, faith in God shines as the overcoming weapon. Faith ultimately gives us the courage to negotiate the twists and turns forced on us by adversity. Raymond McHenry calls it "the adversity principle," a theory that demonstrates well-being is not advantageous to a species. It becomes necessary to wrestle with some form of adversity to gain strength. Adversity can become our friend when we are trained for it. Existence without challenge gives us no character. Adversity triggers the best in us, resulting in both spiritual growth and strength.

There is again some relevance to the maxim that forewarned is forearmed: Did not Jesus forewarn us that adversity is one of the ingredients of life? "I have told you these things so that in me you may have peace. In this world you will have trouble. But take heart, I have overcome the world."[11] When armed with this powerful conviction, it is easier to monitor and adjust to life's troubles.

ADJUSTMENT FOR ACHIEVEMENT

As we revisit Corsini's definition of adjustment, it is important to note his emphasis on "attitudes and behavior." We need this to meet the demands of life effectively. Such attitudes and behavior require the building of what I call the *hope adjustment skill*. This is the conviction that hope is a skill we need to move forward. Hope is an indispensable asset for living.

It is amazing to note the hope at work in Haiti. Haiti is labeled the poorest nation of the Western Hemisphere. In early 2010, this country was struck by a horrific earthquake that resulted in the destruction of 75 percent of Port-au-Prince and several adjacent towns. Some 300,000 people died in the earthquake and its aftermath. One million suffered injuries; thousands had life-altering amputations. Yet these facts don't come near to describing the devastating suffering of the Haitian people. The huge emotional toll that weighs on the minds of Haitians is mind boggling.

Yet Haitians still manage to cultivate a high degree of hope that inspires us. Their determination to move forward despite insurmountable obstacles teaches some vital lessons of the "hope adjustment skill." We can learn from them that hope is nurtured through prayer. After the earthquake, three days of prayer and fasting were proclaimed throughout the country, and Haitians turned out in countless numbers to seek help from above.

Every single day, street vendors show their hope on every street corner. It looks like everybody is selling something. People believe that something good will happen to help them earn their daily bread. Their presence on the streets sends a positive message. Haitians keep hope alive by their fortitude in handling the unimaginable tragedy that was suddenly thrust upon them.

Hope is a steppingstone to achieve things we value in life. It is nurtured through a series of the small deeds we perform as we strive to monitor and adjust to adversity. Though they may seem meaningless, these actions keep us going throughout the day. Consider Sisyphus who was faced with a terrible curse leveled by the Greek gods. Albert Camus, the French philosopher, novelist and essayist, described it as absurd. The gods condemned Sisyphus to ceaselessly roll a boulder to a mountain top just to have it fall back to the bottom. Despite the meaninglessness of this act, Camus saw some meaning: "The struggle itself toward the height is enough to fill a man's heart. One must imagine Sisyphus happy."

Hope is kept alive in action. Albert J. Wells, Jr., in his book *Inspiring Quotations,* gave us a practical list of how hope works in daily routine: Hope "looks for the good in people instead of harping on the worst; it discovers what can be done instead of grumbling about what cannot; it regards problems, large and small, as opportunities; it pushes ahead when it would be easy to quit; it lights up a candle instead of cursing the darkness."[12]

Adjustment is a must. It is imperative to give our inner resources to make the best of the situation. The alternative is just not worth it. Maladjustment has too high a price. It is reassuring to know that our inner resources can always be boosted by power from God. When our values and our spiritual resources are aligned with God, we are equipped to meet all the demands of this life.

NOTES

1. Raymond J. Corsini, *The Dictionary of Psychology* (Ann Arbor, Mich.I: Braun-Brumfield, 1999), 20.
2. Hebrews 6:9.
3. Philippians 2:3-4.
4. I John 4:18.
5. Og Mandigo, "Og Mandigo Quotes," *Thinkexist.com,* thinkexist.com/quotation. access date 2/11/2013
6. Songs 8:6-7.
7. I Corinthians 13:7-8.
8. Romans 15:7.
9. Thomas Hughes, Thomas Hughes Quotes, *Think exist.com,* http//thinkexist.com/quotation/blessed., access date 2/11/2013.
10. Genesis 37:10.
11. John 16:33.
12. Albert M. Wells, Jr., *Inspiring Quotations* (Nashville: Thomas Nelson Publishers, 1988), 90.

Part Two

EMPOWERED FOR A CHANGING WORLD

Chapter Four

Grace for All Seasons

There is a time for everything, and a season for every activity under heaven. (Ecclesiastes 3:1)

Change, the inevitable force affecting every one of us, is markedly noticeable at all levels of our life's journey. Developmental psychology determines the amount of time we should expect to live. It helps us comprehend the changes that take place from conception to death. By the same token, it allows for a greater understanding of the processes that account for these changes.

    The various developmental stages from birth to death correspond to both our chronological age and our psychological development. For simplicity's sake, let's settle on the four major stages: childhood, adolescence, adulthood, and old age. Our objective simply highlights the changes we all undergo in a lifetime. Each level has its share of trials, conflicts, and stressful events. We are blessed when we become aware of divine grace to help us monitor and adjust to every stage for our optimal well-being. These four stages are similar to the four seasons of nature.

SPRINGTIME

I think everyone is very fond of spring. I know I am, probably due to my not so enjoyable experience with the wintry mix of the Northeast. Indeed, winter is usually an unpleasant season with its snow and ice and freezing rain. How can I forget the many falls I have taken on the ice and my frightening adventures driving on snow-covered roads? Spring naturally comes as a heuristic transition I usually anticipate. I look forward to spring. It is wonderful to experience the rebirth spring brings to the surrounding landscape. The lovers of the Song of Songs seized on this opportunity to enjoy spring's beauty. What an enticing invitation the lover made to his beloved to go outside:

> Arise, my darling, my beautiful one, and come with me.
> See! The winter is past; the rains are over and gone.
> Flowers appear on the earth;
> The season of singing has come.[1]

Spring's marvelous regenerating effect is frequently likened to the dawn of life. The first stage of human development begins with all the hopes and potentials of a bright future. Developmental psychology suggests the process begins even with the unborn child who hears during the last trimester of pregnancy and remembers what was heard. If that is the case, we should start helping our child's development even at this early stage through love, education, prayer, and important values. When all conditions work positively, life does blossom in joyful ways.

DIVINE GRACE FOR CHILDHOOD

History demonstrates the availability of divine grace for the early stage of life. The childhood of Moses, for instance, stands as an illustration. He came into the world at a critical time in Israel's history. The Egyptians were taking steps to crush the prosperous advances of the Israelites. As their influence increased, the Egyptians perceived the Israelites as a national security threat. Throughout the land, the Egyptians did what they could to reduce any Israelite population explosion by ordering midwives to kill all baby boys at the moment of birth. This was the time Jochebed gave birth to her son and called him Moses.

Far from allowing the Egyptians to kill her son, Jochebed did some monitoring and adjusting. She managed the situation in such a way as to guarantee the safety of Moses. With the help of her daughter Miriam, she pushed her creative button to use a safe means: a papyrus basket was constructed for her son. The basket was placed in the reeds of the Nile River.

Pharaoh's daughter discovered Moses among the reeds. She soon became the unlikely means not just for his survival but also for his education and training. Moses would one day liberate his enslaved people.

It is remarkable that divine grace protected this baby from the imminent threats against his life. Grace is not simply the unmerited favor of God's protection and guidance, but it is also the inspiration we receive at every stage to take the most plausible steps and the power to travel the surest paths. Grace must have led Jochebed to take this unprecedented measure.

Childhood is a season of complete dependency. Children cannot monitor the reality of their environment. They are especially vulnerable to the physical and social forces of their society. Yet divine grace covers our well-being for all seasons.

Jesus devoted much of his attention to little children. His disciples tried to drive them from his presence so that only the adults would hear his teachings. Jesus rebuked them, stating, "Let the little children come to me, and do not hinder them, for the kingdom of heaven belongs to such as these."[2] Jesus shows us the importance of childhood by bestowing his love on children. Could there ever be any more potent way of teaching children than through the provision of love? Jesus demonstrates that love by the time he spent healing the children around him. He cared both for their physical, mental, and spiritual well-being.

SUMMER

Spring soon gives way to summer and its different outlooks. A new developmental stage brings the freedom, spontaneity, and wonderful opportunities of youth and challenges them to change our communities and our world. What a privilege it is to monitor and adjust our every move so we might make the most of our potentials. The wise man of Ecclesiastes makes it so real for us when he says, "There is a time for everything, a season for every activity under heaven."[3] The ability to monitor and adjust time for our profit, growth, and development is most important. We must make sure our time is invested with our friends and not our enemies.

GRACE FOR YOUTH SEASON

The life of David is a good source for evidence of God's grace for young people. That was a time when Saul became a discredited leader and was to be replaced. The Lord asked Samuel to anoint the new leader.

Samuel's visit to the house of Jesse triggered the highest suspense. For no one, not even Samuel, knew beforehand who was going to be crowned. While most believed Jesse's older sons would win based on their stature and experience, the Lord's choice was on the young David who was not even present. He was brought home and was crowned king as ordered by the Lord. From that day on, the Spirit of the Lord anointed young David with power.

David's power yielded amazing fruit. He courageously faced the fears and stressful events of the battlefield. He fulfilled God's promise of building Israel into a prosperous people. With David at the helm, the nation blossomed to its height of power.

PRODIGALITY

All young men and women can take the necessary steps to become like David. Yet their quest for freedom often results in negative and unpleasant consequences. Consider the story of the Prodigal Son. Once there lived a young man who squandered his father's inheritance by making poor choices. He traveled to a distant country looking for adventure but instead lived an unexpected nightmare. In that foreign land, his evil ways brought him to the edge of financial and moral ruin. Soon he became penniless and hungry, and had to settle for the job of feeding pigs. At his lowest moment, "he came to his senses."[4] He returned home and received the warmest of welcomes from his loving and compassionate father.

A lot of his adventures are part of growing up. Three recent presidents of the United States admitted to the use of illegal drugs. Bill Clinton, George W. Bush, and Barak Obama confessed they had tried marijuana. Once they come to their senses, they were able to make adjustment and find a better lifestyle.

Barack Obama was probably more forthcoming about his use of illicit drugs. He reached a point in his life where he confessed, "I had learned not to care."[5] During his last two years in high school, he risked self-destruction by indulging in both pot and liquor. Communication had broken with his father. He developed a relaxed attitude toward his studies. Eventually his grades began to slip. His problems were compounded by his mixed identity. Being of biracial parents, he could not choose his mother's or his father's identity. He finally accepted himself as an African American.

Like the biblical prodigal, young Obama monitored his life to make the adjustment. He came to his senses, declaring: "I want to make amends."[6] He was able to change course by getting into better physical shape running three miles a day and fasting on Sundays. He applied himself to his studies. His decision to make amends carried him to the honor of being the first black president of the United States.

God helps us and transforms reckless lives. Those who embrace God's word can quickly discover he is the link to a new world of possibilities. To everyone he extends the opportunity of a second chance to monitor and make appropriate adjustments. At the center of God's word stands the great promise of the ability to make amends. One can become a brand new creation with all its benefits and opportunities.

POSITIVE PROPHECY

The psalmist describes "positive prophecy" as a belief in which "our sons in their youth will be like well-nurtured plants and our daughters will be like pillars carved to adorn a palace."[7] The Christian writer Laurie Beth Jones suggests positive prophecy is a divine message that has an influence on behavior.

I was born in a country village. I went to a two-room rural school. Like all the others of my age, my future was supposed to be limited by the scant educational opportunity offered at the school. The turning point for my life took place when I was about twelve years old. The teacher/principal told me I was a smart student with a bright future. He was so sure of it he urged my father to send me to Port-au-Prince to further my education. My father listened to his recommendation, opening a new world of opportunities for me.

In Port-au-Prince, I continued to look back at my younger years and picture my gracious neighbor Lucienne, who predicted that I would one day be somebody. Other people in my congregation also provided me with many encouraging words about a potentially bright future. I knew then I had to dedicate myself to my studies to prove them right. That is still an important reason for my desire to excel in all my endeavors.

God's positive prophecies for young people are backed up by his power to make them a reality. He calls us to embrace a higher ethical behavior in tune with the timeless and proven laws he has given us to help us with our activities. The book of Proverbs lays out some practical guidelines to develop and build the character of young people. It seeks to help develop them "for attaining wisdom and discipline; for understanding words of insight; for acquiring a disciplined and prudent life, doing what is right and just and fair; for giving prudence to the simple, knowledge and discretion to young."[8]

This kind of teaching also extends to relationship building. Wisdom urges the young to respect their parents. "Listen to your father, who gave you life, and do not despise your mother when she is old."[9] Young people are called to contribute to the well-being of their parents. "May your father and mother be glad; may she who gives you birth rejoice."[10] When put into practice, such teaching reinforces love and brings harmony to family relationships for the benefit of both parent and child.

When anchored in God's word, this wisdom is available to those who wish to manage their lives effectively. Young people are advised to monitor the situations of their lives and adjust even at their young age. When young Timothy followed Paul's guidance, he was able to become a mature spiritual leader. Paul taught him to let no one "look down upon you because you are young, but set an example for the believers in speech, in faith and purity."[11] It is even possible to shine in one's youth.

AUTUMN

The signs of nature's cyclical changes are clearly marked. Trees change color in the autumn. The flowers of spring and summer wilt and die. The air turns chilly. We cannot escape the coming weather change. Time moves on.

Just as time moves on, so do our developmental processes. The fall of life is likened to a declining adulthood ushering the unstoppable signs of dying. By and large, the physical body reflects this chronological season of life. Our attention is primarily focused on the mental and spiritual transition. Paul undoubtedly was very conscious of this transition. "When I was a child," he confessed, "I talked like a child, I thought like a child, and I reasoned like a child. When I became a man, I put childish ways behind me."[12] Manhood or womanhood requires a shift to higher ground. We ought to monitor our thoughts and adjust them to this new reality to enjoy full-fledged maturity.

Such maturity is the steppingstone to fulfilling our mission. Make no mistake that we are here under heaven for a purpose. When we stand in God's presence and power, our talents are used properly to advance humanity. We have the assurance that, like the righteous of the first psalm, "whatever he does prospers."[13] We gain confidence despite life's uncertainties. We know we can monitor each situation and adjust to it for our ultimate purpose.

WINTER

The winter of life is old age: the ultimate stage of a full lifespan. Just as winter destroys nature's summer beauty, old age sucks away our physical stamina and energy. Pierre de Ronsard, a French Renaissance poet, compared the change to a withered flower. He invited Cassandra, a fictional lover, to pay a visit to the rose that had just blossomed like a purple sundress. On reaching the site, they unfortunately discovered the rose's demise. The poet wrote the following advice to his lover:

So if you believe me, my sweet,
While you are blossoming
Still fresh and green
Harvest your youth:
For like this flower old age
Will blight your beauty.[14]

There is no stage of life that requires closer attention and adjustment skills than the winter of life. We must be ready for major adjustments so we can make the best of our aging beauty, energy, and mental sharpness. It shall become clear that we have to prepare to leave this world. We are well instructed that "death is the destiny of every man; the living should take this to heart."[15]

People seek to manage the stress and uncertainties of winter in a thousand and one ways. Some make preliminary funeral arrangements. Back in Haiti, I recall when my grandfather had a sepulcher built for his burial. He must have been in his sixties when he took that extraordinary measure. As he kept on living, his likeness for this particular sepulcher waned. Later, he went on to build a better one before he died in his nineties. Others have the wisdom to draw up a will describing provisions for their possessions.

People seek to put the final touch on their legacy. This ultimate effort is like the Mute Swan that remains quiet until the moment just before it dies. It then sings its only beautiful song. A classic example is Brahm's final work, *Four Serious Songs*, written before his death at the age of sixty-three. He must have had a premonition he was going to die, just as Mozart did when he wrote his *Requiem*. Whatever the circumstances, God's grace is available during the winter of life as it is in the first three seasons. The psalmist provides an assurance when he proclaims the righteous "will bear fruit in old age. They will stay fresh and green."[16] Psychologist Dean Simonton believes that even in the very last year of life, "a sudden burst of creative vitality can emerge." Evidently it is impossible to determine this last year of life despite the signs pointing to the end game. Yet it must be an abundantly great feeling to reach life's termination with a sense of fulfillment realizing that your life mission is fulfilled. Paul experienced that feeling when he exclaimed, "I have fought the good fight, I have finished the race, I have kept the faith."[17]

GRACE FOR ALL WALKS OF LIFE

God's grace is available as the ever-present staying power to help us handle the trials of life. Such grace reaches out to people of all walks of life. There is no way to define with precision this productive bracket. Some achieve greatness early in the summer of life. Mozart composed more than six hundred unique musical works including masses, concerts, symphonies, sonatas, operas, and so on by the time he died in his mid-thirties. He was composing symphonies when he was nine.

What matters is to cultivate the awareness of the presence and the power of God in all things and at all times. God's grace was available for Paul as he was engaged in a vibrant ministry to the Gentile world. In the midst of his missionary activities, he became afflicted by a condition that affected him deeply, one he humbly described as "a thorn in the flesh." Despite this setback, he was able to gather enough strength to continue on his mission through the availability of God's grace: "My grace was sufficient for you, for my power is made perfect in weakness."[18]

Grace is God's power for hard times. John Newton knew something about the reality of that grace. As a youngster, he followed in his father's profession and became a seafarer. Eventually, he became a slave captain engaged in the transporting of African slaves to the New World. Newton had a lackluster career, being flogged and losing his rank in the British Navy while trying to escape the service. Yet his experience reached a turning point during a storm while aboard the *Greyhound* in 1748. The ship almost sank. He awoke in the middle of the night and called out to God as the vessel was filling up with water, "Lord, have mercy on me." That night, Newton was saved and spent the rest of his life working for God. He praised God's grace in his moving hymn, "Amazing Grace," still one of the most favored of Christian hymns:

> Thro' many dangers, toils, and snares
> I have already come
> 'Tis grace hath brought me safe thus far
> And grace will lead me home.

The expression "all walks of life" describes every occupation and profession including the lofty: Paul as the missionary and John Newton as the social outcast. It extends to those in all social hierarchies we create to separate people. God's grace is readily available to help all manage stressful events effectively. We can grow through any traumatic event to enjoy productive and meaningful living.

NOTES

1. Song of Songs 2:10-12.
2. Mathew 19:14.
3. Ecclesiastes 3:1.

4. Luke 15:17.
5. Barack Obama, *Dreams from My Father* (New York: Three Rivers Press, 1995), 93.
6. Obama, *Dreams from My Father*, 119.
7. Psalm 144:12.
8. Proverbs 1:2-4.
9. Proverbs 23:22.
10. Proverbs 23:25.
11. I Timothy 4:12.
12. I Corinthians 13:11.
13. Psalm 1:3.
14. Pierre de Ronsard, "Ode a Cassandre," *Live Journal*, Funkyturtle.live.journal.com/311495.html., access 2/12/2013.
15. Ecclesiastes 6:12.
16. Psalm 92:14.
17. 2 Timothy 4:7.
18. 2 Corinthians 12:8.

Chapter Five

Anchor for a Changing World

> We have this hope as an anchor for the soul, firm and secure. (Hebrews 6:19)

In 2004, my wife Rozelle and I enjoyed a novel experience when we boarded a Royal Caribbean cruise bound for the West Indies. The ship stopped in the Bahamas, St. Thomas, Puerto Rico, and Haiti. Organized by Haiti Special Project, the project commemorated the two hundredth anniversary of Haitian independence.

We had a marvelous time traveling the open seas for a full week filled with adventure. Our ship was a floating city. It was possible to find everything to meet all our needs—both commercial and recreational. One night we saw a show. A number of restaurants competed for our taste. There was an exercise facility available at all hours. Of course, a large mall offered the allurements of taking advantage of all the sales one missed on land. I was particularly impressed by the size of the ship. It was then the largest ship in the world.

NEED FOR AN ANCHOR

An anchor is a heavy object used to keep ships from floating away, locked to a specific point. The anchor keeps the ship from escaping away from its moorings by the various forces, wind and currents, and the vertical wave movement. The anchor holds the vessel in place in all kinds of weather, including the most severe storms. Every ship, regardless of its size, needs an anchor.

A ship is a metaphor for life. Just as ships travel on wide and vast oceans, exposed to the chaotic mix of changing weathers and unforeseeable storms, so do we. We must monitor and adjust our course to navigate through the troubled and mighty waters. When we are able to make it to shore, we definitely need an anchor to hold us in a secure and stable position. Each one of us must contend with some winds and turbulent currents. Paul reminds us in his letter to the Hebrews, "We have this hope as an anchor for the soul, firm and steadfast."[1] An anchor as firm and secure as hope offers us the power to monitor and manage through all our trials and storms.

One thing that helps us weather these trials and storms is hope. Hope is the invaluable force that arms us for both the struggle of survival and the ability to thrive. Hal Lindsay, American evangelist and Christian writer, suggests, "Man can live about forty days without food, about three days without water, about eight minutes without air... but only for one second without hope."[2]

Hope is what we use to navigate through values to manage the changes that take place in our lives. Hope can withstand all our stormy changes.

AN ANCHOR OF INDIVIDUAL SECURITY

As we look at the world's history, we cannot miss the ongoing but irresistible flow of change. Heraclitus, one of the most prominent philosophers of ancient Greece, prior to Socrates and Plato, developed a philosophy grounded in the very reality of change. For Heraclitus, nothing stays still. He saw the universe in constant change. Heraclitus asserted no man ever steps into the same river twice, for new waters are always flowing.

This flux theory reflects the uncertainties of life. First, uncertainty is a part of life itself. It is foremost in our very constitution. We are reminded of the fragility of life. The Bible compares our bodies to the passing nature of grass, according to the prophet Isaiah: "All men are like grass, and all their glory is like the flowers of the field. The grass withers and the flowers fall."[3] James put it even more bluntly: Human life is like a mist that "appears for a little while and then vanishes."[4]

The many diseases afflicting our bodies remind us of our human frailty. Consider the long list of cancers that can destroy us. It is a continuing battle monitoring and adjusting to the ongoing changes connected with the seasons of life. Hope is a powerful necessity in our struggle to cope. It is possible to find some security through it all. The power of unshakable hope helps us manage the rough waters of our changing times. Hope gives us the wisdom to monitor the changes affecting our body and mind and makes the necessary adjustment to attain more stable condition.

Recently a member of my extended family awoke one day to face an unexpected condition. She did not feel like herself. She was uncomfortable and dizzy. Her vision was blurred. She felt so much discomfort she decided to visit the emergency room. To her surprise, she was diagnosed with diabetes. From that day on, her life was no longer the same. She would require a brand new commitment to monitoring and adjusting herself to cope with this debilitating disease. She now must carefully monitor what she eats and drinks, and adjust the amount she consumes. Yet she is determined, since she has the hope of more fulfilling days ahead of her.

HOPE FOR ONE DAY AT A TIME

Life's uncertainties reveal themselves in the most unexpected and unpredictable situations. Without our power to monitor and adjust, we could easily sink into frustration and disappointment. We must plan, yet we are so often left at the mercies of unforeseen circumstances. For no one can anticipate what will happen tomorrow. The wise man warns us not to "boast about tomorrow, for you don't know what a day may bring forth."[5] It is sheer wisdom to learn to live one day at a time.

John Fitzgerald Kennedy woke up on November 22, 1963, with bright plans. He made the memorable journey to Dallas, Texas. Adoring crowds gathered along his route. Jackie was at his side waving to these crowds. Despite their outlook for a better future, an assassin's bullet changed the course of history.

What is important to remember, the skill to survive the inevitable stress of change, is quite simply hope. I have experienced much success, but I have had a fair number of failures. I have learned to live a day at a time with the mind of Christ. I have built my confidence on the unshakable conviction that "in all things, God works for the good of those who love him, who have been called according to his purpose."[6] This faith remains the motivational force that maintains my resolve and determination to persevere. I believe the conventional wisdom that, "with ordinary talent and extraordinary perseverance, most everything is attainable."

An anchor of inner security is the basic tool for life. It is like the wisdom of building on rock rather than sand. Jesus gave us the parable of the two builders. The wise builder built a strong foundation according to the timeless principles of Christ's word. His house resisted the most violent storms, winds, and rains because its foundation was laid on rock. The second builder watched his house collapse, destroyed by violent storms because its foundation was built on sand. Anyone aware of this story would seek to apply it in all of life's endeavors.

THE ANCHOR OF NATIONAL SECURITY

There is an anchor that lies at the center of the existence and evolution of a nation. Similar to individuals, nations hold onto some special historical developments and fundamental ideals that unite them. Nations go through tough times as well. The storms that hit them come as internal conflicts, civil wars, and even natural disasters. On January 12, 2010, Haiti was hit with a 7.0 ferocious earthquake that practically destroyed the entire country. Besides the death of some three hundred thousand people, the physical and economic infrastructure collapsed as well. Yet its citizens muster an amazing flow of collective hope to keep going.

On the other hand, the United States stands as the example of a nation that has learned to withstand the peril of strong internal storms by relying on the ideals of the founding fathers. These ideals were inscribed in the American Declaration of Independence: "We hold these truths to be self-evident, that all men are created equal, that they are endowed by their Creator, with certain unalienable rights, that among those are life, liberty and the pursuit of happiness." This anchor has held the United States together for more than two centuries, the longest time of any of the world's modern democracies.

Yet the United States has had its share of turbulence. One storm was the crisis brought about by slavery. This oppression runs against the great equality claim of the American Declaration of Independence. In the heyday of plantation slavery, African Americans could not dream of sharing the benefits of freedom. They were denied all the rights of pursuing even the smallest benefits of the American dream. The horrors of slavery led to the fragmentation of this nation into a civil war.

In spite of overwhelming divisions, conflicts, and war, the ideal of the American Declaration of Independence prevailed. It was eloquently reaffirmed in Gettysburg by Abraham Lincoln as he delivered one of the most celebrated speeches, reminding us that this nation was "conceived in liberty, and dedicated to the proposition that all men are created equal." The president said that freedom was the sole anchor of national security.

A century later, America survived another storm. This time it was the civil rights movement. Despite the abolition of slavery and new emerging constitutional rights, segregation and discrimination persisted to keep African Americans as second class citizens for the century that followed the Civil War. Dr. Martin Luther King, Jr., fought for freedom and human dignity on the ideal described by the American Declaration of Independence. This document remains an anchor of that American ideal. Dr. King stood on the rights of freedom for everyone.

THE ANCHOR OF A SOUND MIND

The changes that come our way must be handled and processed effectively. A sound mind is an indispensable anchor for us. It is one of the gifts God gave us to become effective problem solvers. Paul reminds Timothy of his great potential because he was endowed with a spirit of "power, love and a sound mind."[7] Leonard Sweet, in his recently published book *Jesus' Prescription for a Healthy Life,* describes a healthy mental life as one striving for well-being. In his view, Jesus urged us to "mind our thoughts."

As we "mind our thoughts," remember René Descartes' approach. He is considered the father of modern philosophy and a key figure of the modern scientific revolution. In his *Discourse on Method,* he said the only way we can prove our existence is by our ability to think: "I think, therefore I am." This assertion, which has become a fundamental element of Western philosophy, is a tremendous challenge for us to use our cognitive abilities effectively to monitor and adjust to changes in our daily living.

THE ANCHOR OF PREPAREDNESS

Jesus told the story of the Ten Virgins, demonstrating we need to be ready at all times. In this case, it was preparedness to meet the bridegroom. Five of these virgins were foolish while the other five were wise. The test was to have light available before the arrival of the bridegroom. The wise ones took their lamps with enough oil on hand. The others had lamps without oil. Eventually, when the bridegroom came, only the virgins who had demonstrated soundness of mind were able to meet him.

The story reminds us of the close connection between preparedness and wisdom. Solomon defines wisdom as "doing what is right and just and fair."[8] He associates wisdom with a sense of discipline. The discipline of wisdom is an anchor for proper adjustment. Wisdom endows us with a sense of timing. The wise virgins knew how to use time effectively. The anchor of preparedness helps us plan and prepare for all eventualities and possibilities coming our way.

THE ANCHOR OF STABILITY

We have emphasized the reality of the ongoing change we face in our everyday life. These changes also stem from the steady progress of technology.

We must recognize the rapid change in our cultural and social mores. The social process spreads at such a fast pace it is difficult to keep up. We have to know that despite foundational shifts, our anchor holds, an anchor grounded in the mind of Christ.

The person who survives and thrives in our changing world is the one with a mental attitude grounded in spiritual stability. This person is able to withstand the changes, standing firm. The mind of Christ allows us to be most responsive to change.

More than anything else, we need to move hand in hand with change. As a matter of fact, it is not a farfetched idea to make change our friend. Technology, for instance, expands our communication ability exponentially. With this new communication ability, we have a strategy to embrace the reality that we are also changing. It is imperative to be ready to renew ourselves daily to adjust these changes to maximize our well-being.

NURTURING HOPE

The eagle is the king of the predator birds, known for its majestic and powerful flight. The eagle inspires us by its ability to renew itself through what is known as "eagle molting." It is a process that helps to keep hope alive in the darkest of circumstances.

After living more than thirty years, eagles began to lose their feathers. Their beaks and claws are altered. During that time, they walk like turkeys. They have lost their strength to fly. The molting eagle finds itself in a valley. It is a down time during which eagles lose even the desire to eat.

Then another phenomenon takes place when the eagle retreats to a mountain range where it is directly exposed to the sun. It is the most dramatic stage in the life of eagles. They either renew themselves or die. As the bird peers into the sun, it regains its strength. Those who survive this experience fly away as young as a new eagle, with another thirty to forty years of life.

Life takes each of us to a similar valley-and-peak experience. By keeping hope alive, we can be like the eagle that can both molt and be renewed. What is important is that hope is maintained through our activity. As we move forward, we take all necessary steps to progress and advance. I have in recent years developed these three principles of excellence that helps me keep hope alive by being my best, doing my best, and expect God's best.

BE YOUR BEST

Let us begin with the sports technique called "peak performance." This technique is used to describe an individually based development and mentoring approach designed to raise the performance of individuals. Athletes train to perform at their peak, at their highest possible level in their best physical state. Based on the sport, special equipment and clothing are marketed to help athletes reach the top of their skills. Peak performance is also used by corporations to motivate employees to seek maximum performance. In whatever field, the strategy is to help the individual bury his limits and be raised to higher levels.

Before we can ever do our best, the first step is motivation. God gives us the potential to be our best: "For I am the Lord your God who teaches you what is best for you, who direct you in the way you should go."[9] We become our best by walking in the direction God has set out for us. It takes a definite level of commitment. The Bible teaches the way to go to reach this peak performance: "Build yourselves up in your most holy faith and pray in the Holy Spirit."[10] In his book *The Seven Habits of Highly Effective People*, Steven Covey shows us that private victory precedes public victory. Only a self built on the bedrock of God's principles allows us to reach our peak performance in our environment.

DO YOUR BEST

The story is told of a carpenter who was about to retire. His contractor commissioned him the task of building one final house before packing up his tools. The carpenter was consumed with thoughts of his retirement and basked in the glow of his past performance. He was not motivated by any idea of peak performance. His heart was not in his work.

As a result, he invested little of his experience in the construction. His workmanship was shoddy. He used inferior materials. It was an unfortunate way to end his career. When the carpenter finished his work and the builder came to inspect the house, the contractor handed the front-door key to the carpenter. "This is your house," he said, "my gift to you."

What a shock! What a shame! If he had only known he was building his own house, he would have done it differently. Now he had to live in the home he had built poorly. We should be driven by the principle of excellence. Excel in whatever you do. The Bible teaches us: "Whatever you do, work at with all your heart as working for the Lord, not for men."[11]

EXPECT GOD'S BEST

It is imperative we keep in mind that our victory ultimately lies with God. The psalmist expressed this principle with his unshakable conviction: "Some trust in chariots and some in horses, but we trust in the name of the Lord our God." [12] The very thought of knowing that God is part of the process of whatever you do implies positive results. You should be persuaded that God knows what is best for you. Second, that conviction builds up your confidence. As we sail the seas of life, we should bear in mind that God "is able to do immeasurably more than all we ask or imagine according to his power that is at work within us."[13] Anchored with God's unchangeable love, we can move with confidence from victory to victory.

NOTES

1. Hebrews 6:19.
2. Hal Lindsay, quoted in Wells' Inspiring Quotations, 90.
3. Isaiah 40:6.
4. James 4:14.
5. Proverbs 27:1.
6. Romans 8:28.
7. I Timothy 1:7 KJV.
8. Proverbs 1: 3.
9. Isaiah 48:17.
10. Jude 1:20.
11. Colossians 3:23.
12. Psalm 20: 7.
13. Ephesians 3:20.

Chapter Six

Managing the Stress of Time

> Be careful, then, how you live-not as unwise but as wise, making the most of every opportunity. (Eph. 5: 15)

Modern man is slipping into a time pressure cooker. Dr. Richard Swenson talks about how the reality of time pressure is real to all of us. "We talk of no time, lack of time, not enough time, or being out of time."[1] How many times have we heard people complain that "there are not enough hours in the day"? Others bemoan the fact there is "so much to do and not enough time." We live busy if not overloaded lives. The promise that technology would yield more leisure time is now seen as a mere utopia. Years ago, a poll by Yankelovich and Clancy Shulman found that seventy-three percent of women complained of having too little leisure time. Fifty-one percent of men had that same complaint. Yet time pressure has proved disastrous for our health. It is important to make every effort to monitor and adjust to time to live a stress-free life.

TIME-CONSCIOUSNESS

For millennia, time has been a free commodity. For our prehistoric ancestors, time flew past, nameless and in no particular order. In fact time has remained a mystery that we have not even been able to define. During the Middle Ages Augustine weighed in regarding this difficulty of defining time: "I know well enough what (time) is, provided that nobody asks me; but if I am asked what it is and tried to explain it, I am baffled."[2]

It is certain that our attitude toward the use of time as a means to achieve goals has changed. This utilitarian approach led to the whole endeavor of measuring and organizing time. The Babylonians began by establishing a seven-day week. Later, horology, the invention of clocks, accelerated this process. When the Greeks invented water clocks as a way of keeping track of time, the effect of time on our lives had changed forever. This particular clock measured time as the amount of water that drained from a filled tank. It lasted through the Roman and Arab civilizations. When the French invented mechanical clocks, there was no escaping time as a finite measurement. Today clocks and watches are highly accurate mechanisms that keep track of our every movement.

Technological advances have put a host of instruments that monitor time at our disposal. These gadgets not only make us more aware of the passage of time but also the impact of time on our lives. Personally I rarely escape the reality of time consciousness. From the moment I awaken in the morning, until I sleep at night, the effect of time jumps at me.

As I make it from the bedroom to the garage, I am aware there are clocks everywhere. A clock is visible from every room of my house. A grandfather clock prominently hangs on the wall in the living room. A VCR nearby also ticks tirelessly to remind me of the flow of time. In the kitchen, time is kept not just on the stove but also on the microwave just above the stove. On my way to the garage, I observe right over my desk yet another clock. The dashboard of the car displays the time as well. Besides these, my time consciousness is further reinforced by the silver watch I wear on my left arm and the cell phone I keep in my pocket.

CONQUERING THE STRESS OF TIME

The process of organizing, measuring, and technologizing time has contributed to the increased pressure in our lives. In 2004, a telephone survey of 790 respondents suggested that "time pressure is significantly associated with distress for men and women."[3] A majority of us are burdened by overloaded lives driven by clocks.

An example of this overloading is that people overwork. Take the case of Jeannie, for instance. She gets up by five in the morning to get to her job at a Pittsburgh hospital by seven. Many times, she is asked to stay for a second shift. When she finally gets home after nine at night, she has no energy left. She complains of fatigue. People work nonstop every day, weekends, and even holidays. Some work two and sometimes three jobs while others moonlight. Everywhere the pressure for greater productivity and higher profit drives us.

Technology contributes a lot toward increasing the stress of time. New gadgets emerge daily that bring us innovation as well as stress. The computer, for instance, is one of the most marvelous tools at our disposal. While it helps improve our work performance, it can also be quite frustrating, as anyone knows when there is a system crash.

REST

There is a well-known maxim suggesting we work to live rather than live to work. Rest is a good practice that helps us renew ourselves from overwork. God provides us with a great example through his action at the time of Creation, an event totally immersed in time. He brought the earth into being in six days. Every act from the creation of light to the creation of man in his image and likeness took place within that timeframe. On the seventh day, designated as the Sabbath, God rested.

The lesson is clear for us. For our own good health and well-being, we are also asked to conquer the stress of time by cultivating an awareness of time. We must learn to budget time more effectively to accomplish the tasks put before us.

It is imperative we heed the law of observing the Sabbath of rest. "Six days you shall labor and do all your work, but the seventh day is a Sabbath to the Lord your God. On it you shall not do any work."[4] Time must be devoted to rest and proper sleeping. Dr. Roberta Lee explains that sleep deprivation affects health. People who are sleep deprived can "experience attention lapses, reduced short-term memory capacity, impaired judgment…"[5] We can conquer the stress time continually brings into our lives by abiding by the divine principle of rest. Time must be monitored and adjusted for our own welfare.

INVESTING THE TIME

The issue that faces us is one of balance. Since it is unhealthy to be overbooked and overscheduled, we must seek a way to take control of time instead of being controlled by it. The best strategy to manage stress is by investing properly the time at our disposal. Sound biblical teaching tells us how we can wisely manage time to enjoy a meaningful and productive life. That is the significance of Paul's call to the Ephesians to "make the most of every opportunity."[6] We are familiar with this biblical principle that "if a man will not work, he shall not eat."[7]

Charles Wesley provides us with an example of someone who made the best use of his time. He was born in England as the eighteenth of nineteen children of Samuel and Susannah Wesley. Though he lived in the shadow of his more prominent brother John, his contribution to the newly born Methodist movement cannot be overlooked. As both a creative poet and inspired musician, he wrote the hymns that animated the new movement. Charles had an obsession that set him apart as an excellent manager of time. It is said he averaged ten poetic lines a day over a period of fifty years. In fifty-three years he published fifty volumes accounting for 8,989 hymns.

Like Wesley, we are called to live in a meaningful and productive way. One of the great purposes of education is to train us to become productive citizens and contribute to our personal welfare and to society at large. Wesley's achievement reminds us that "we have different gifts according to the grace given us."[8] His extraordinary example stands as a great catalyst as we seek our own path of achievement.

OPPORTUNITY

One definition of opportunity is "an appropriate or favorable time or occasion." Opportunity intersects with time. In this merging with time, opportunity becomes the meaningful avenue to accomplish a specific goal. Saying this in another way, it is like being at the right time at the right place.

We must always keep an eye open to catch opportunities. When I first arrived in the United States, I knew I wanted to further my education even though I did not have the resources to pay for my academic studies. A door opened when my Pittsburgh friends called to let me know about a scholarship at Pittsburgh Theological Seminary. This became the opportunity of a lifetime.

Zaccheus made the most of his opportunity when he met Jesus. He had an inner urge to see Jesus because of what he heard of Jesus. When the moment arrived, a crowd surrounded Jesus, blocking Zaccheus' view. He had to monitor and adjust by climbing a sycamore tree just to see Jesus. While Zaccheus did his best, God did the rest. Zaccheus found salvation as the end result of his effort to connect with Jesus.

Opportunity came to Zaccheus. If opportunity fails to knock at our doors, we can also go and knock at its door. We have to look for an opportunity. Should we need a job, we peruse the newspapers, navigate the Internet, visit the employment office, and talk to anyone who might have an opportunity for us. We prepare ourselves by sharpening our tools. Long ago the Roman philosopher Seneca said, "Luck is what happens when preparation meets opportunity." It takes careful monitoring to make the most of our opportunity.

TIME MANAGEMENT

Once again let's look at Aesop's stories to illustrate the appropriateness of time management. The race between the hare and the tortoise is the story I am thinking of. The hare teased the tortoise for being slow. To save face the tortoise challenged the hare to a race that he pledged to win. The fox, who was engaged as the referee, set the course for them. When the time came, both hare and tortoise started off together, but the hare was soon so far ahead that he thought he might as well have a rest. So down he lay and fell asleep. Meanwhile, the tortoise kept plodding on, and in time reached the finished line. When the hare woke up and dashed to the finish line, he discovered the tortoise had already won the race.

Though all the potential of organizing and measuring time is readily available, we don't take advantage of it. The challenge remains to devise the best strategy to become effective time managers. The hare in Aesop's story had the capability of winning the race. But because he lacked time management skills he ended up losing.

Solomon reflected on time management, concluding through experience, "There is a time for everything under the heaven, a season for every activity. A time to be born and a time to die, a time to plant and a time to uproot, a time to kill and a time to heal, a time to tear down and a time to build, a time to weep and a time to laugh, a time to mourn and a time to dance..."[9] The list of activities goes on.

Several lessons stem from Solomon's reflection. First of all, it is a call for better time management. Given the standard span of time at our disposal, computed by the psalmist as three score and ten, we definitely must come to the understanding of using the time at our disposal effectively to achieve our life goals. We must be good time managers.

Second, it is clear we have no control over time when it comes down to life's events. No one can determine the time of their birth and death. We must learn to monitor and adjust by making the most of the timeframe and space we are divinely allotted. Considering the unmistaken impact time and space exert on our lives, this factor has huge consequences.

Third, we must use our wisdom to take control of those activities we can control. Such a commitment calls us to be responsible to live and be engaged in our world and communities as useful and productive citizens. William Barclay says in his commentary of the Gospel of Matthews that "human beings are born for greatness." What a beautiful challenge to answer the call of greatness.

History has many examples of individuals who rose to change their world without coming close to the psalmist's goal of three score and ten. Martin

Luther King managed his time by applying himself to make the most of his opportunities. He understood the first season of life was to be dedicated to education. He was only thirty-nine years old when he died. Yet he made such an impact on this nation that the United States Congress has honored him as the only African American with a national holiday.

GOAL-SETTING

Effective time management cannot be conceived or achieved without some perspective of setting goals. What matters here is, the process of establishing specific future objectives or end-results that provide: a) a basis for motivation, b) an estimation of the amount of effort to expend and c) guidelines or cues to determine if one is moving toward the desired end-result."

Goal setting bids us to recognize the close interrelationship between time and change. As time advances, the reality around us changes as well. That is why we need to monitor time and make appropriate adjustments.

JESUS—THE PERFECT TIME MANAGER

Our efforts to manage time better must be highly inspired by Jesus' timeless example. His great mission from His Father was the saving of the human race. He knew he had just three years to fulfill this lofty mission. To do this, he needed to make the best of time available. That's the meaning of his statement: "As long as it is day, we must do the work of him who sent me. Night is coming when no one can work."[10]

To fulfill this mission, Jesus displayed magnificently the great time management principles that common sense commands us to emulate. These principles revolve around the concepts of purpose, priorities, and planning.

First, Jesus was driven by a single-minded purpose of a mission of salvation and the welfare of humankind. He proclaimed he came so that men and women "may have life and have it to the full."[11] His time was wholeheartedly devoted to this very purpose as seen in his ministry of teaching, preaching, and healing.

To fulfill his mission, Jesus saw the need to set priorities. While his contemporaries would surround themselves with the insatiable quest of materialism and hedonism, Jesus directed them to higher values. He bid them to prioritize the things worth having: "Seek first the kingdom of God and his righteousness, and all these things will be given to you as well."[12]

Finally, Jesus, the great time manager, coordinated his activities with good planning. When called to act on behalf of his friend Lazarus, time consciousness was indeed present: "Are there not twelve hours of daylight? A man who walks by day will not stumble, for he sees by this world light."[13]

A day in the life of Jesus reflects the coordination of these time management skills with his mission. At dawn, when the rooster crowed, Jesus began the day with prayer. He set the tone for his day by seeking the will of his Father. During the rest of his day, he reached out to his people. Matthew summarized the essential activities of Jesus' day by writing that he "went throughout Galilee teaching in the synagogue, preaching the good news and healing every sickness and disease among the people."[14] Jesus made the most opportunity of his life by using his time helping others and serving as an example for the rest of us. There lays the whole meaning and purpose for living.

WISDOM

It is true science and technologies have perfected the mechanism of measuring and monitoring time, but time is best managed by using our wisdom. We are much wiser when we see time in the light of eternity. Simply put, our time here is limited. Yet beyond time there is eternity.

Despite all the monitoring and adjusting we achieve, time will win the contest. Just as we were born in time, we are bound to die in the very same fashion. Moses wrote the ninetieth psalm highlighting that very message: "The length of our days is seventy years-or eighty, if we have the strength; yet their span is but trouble and sorrow, for they quickly pass and we fly away."[15] It sounds like a death sentence concocted by time against us, a sentence against which there is just no appeal. While this is true, there is also some negotiation we can make with time.

In the end, the psalmist's recommendation is worth taking with utmost consideration: "Teach us to number our days aright that we may gain a heart of wisdom."[16] Wisdom helps us to negotiate with time. By accepting our fate, we are vested with the best attitude and stand in the most strategic position to make the best of each new opportunity.

NOTES

1. Richard A. Swenson, M.D., Margin: Restoring Emotional, Physical, Financial and Time Reserves to Overloaded Lives (Colorado Springs, Colo.: Navpress, 1992).

2. Augustine, "A matter of Time," *Oracle Think Quest*, Library.thinkquest.org/06aug01010/presentExistence.htlm., access 2/12/2013.

3. Susan Roxburgh, Journal of Health and Social Behavior, June 2004, vol. 45, issue 2.
4. Exodus 20:9-10.
5. Roberta Lee, Superstress Solution (New York: Random House, 2010), 36.
6. Ephesians 5:16.
7. 2 Thessalonians 3: 10.
8. Romans 12: 6.
9. Ecclesiastes 3: 1-3.
10. John 9:4.
11. John 10:10.
12. Matthew 6:32.
13. John 11:9.
14. Matthew 4:23.
15. Psalm 90:10.
16. Psalm 90:12.

Part Three

EMPOWERED AS A CHANGE AGENT

Chapter Seven

Managing Your Health in a Changing World

I pray that you may enjoy good health and that all may go well with you, even as your soul is getting along well. (3 John 2)

Mens Sana in Corpore Sano (A Healthy Mind in a Healthy Body)

We live in a changing world. Everything around us changes at every moment. Technological progress is again at the forefront. The dizzying speed of technology has left many people behind, particularly the older generation. Though I can make my computer work, I am conscious of falling behind daily.

Most conspicuous is the impact of stress that comes from this ever increasing change. Alvin Toffler identified this stress as "future shock." He describes it as "the shattering stress and disorientation that we induce in individuals by subjecting them to too much change in too short a time."[1]

More recently, Dr. Roberta Lee observed the current magnitude of stress we experience, calling it "SUPERSTRESS." She refers to it as "layers and layers piled atop one another so subtly that sometimes we don't even notice what's happening."[2]

This high level of stress has a negative impact on our physical and psychological system. It is important to take steps to monitor and adjust this impact of change so we can enjoy a healthy and happy life.

THE QUEST FOR WELL-BEING

Everyone seeks equilibrium. That is normal. In his *Dictionary of Psychology*, Raymond Corsini defines our well-being as a subjective state that includes "happiness, self-esteem, and life satisfaction." Long ago, Jabez from I

Chronicles prayed for his well-being: "Oh that you would bless me and extend my territory. Let your hand be with me, and keep me from harm so that I will be free from pain."[3] During the twentieth century, Sigmund Freud, in his book *Civilization and Its Discontent,* suggests that we seek pleasure and avoid pain in our search for this well-being. Yet our quest for well-being is often diverted by the heavy stress that overwhelms our lives and jeopardizes our health.

Health stands at the very center of this much coveted state of well-being. Let us for the moment look at the concept of health. The World Health Organization defines it as "a state of complete physical, mental and social well-being, and not merely the absence of disease or infirmity." Health is central in God's plan for our well-being. The book of Proverbs points to God's commands as the clearest and most direct pathway to health. "Do not let them out of your sight; for they are life to those who find them and health to a man's whole body."[4] Considering the beauty and prominent value of health, we have a sacred duty to nurture and maintain our health.

It is unfortunate that men and women engage in their quest for good health in the wrong places. To deal with stress, people have resorted to highly addictive and dangerous pills that prove more harmful than beneficial. A recent *Los Angeles Times* analysis of government data uncovered the abuse of prescription narcotics overdoses. These drugs, which include Oxycontin®, Vicotin®, Valium®, and others, are used as painkillers and as a relief for anxiety. The *Times* analysis compared the number of narcotic overdose deaths with those by motor vehicle accidents in 2009. It found that drug-related deaths exceeded vehicular deaths by at least 37,485 people nationwide.[5]

PROMISED HEALTH

We require the existence of a well-designed divine plan for our health. God seeks to provide us with a total health package that includes our physical, emotional, and spiritual welfare. He made that provision for the entire Israelite community during their pilgrimage to the Promised Land. "Worship the Lord your God and his blessing will be on your food and water. I will take away sickness from among you... I will give you a full life span."[6]

This promise is strengthened in a letter from the apostle John to his beloved friend Gaius: "I pray that you may enjoy good health and that all may go well with you, even as your soul is getting along well."[7]

The promise of a full lifespan, though very attractive, unfortunately falls on deaf ears. We know over the years that health management has made some impressive progress. The infectious diseases that once plagued the human race have been brought under control. The nearest departments of public health in any major cities have a battery of the vaccines available to ward off common viruses and infectious diseases that used to trigger a death sentence. Yet we also know there has emerged what Dr. Richard Swenson identified as a new morbidity. It is connected with our irresponsible lifestyles that allow us to make choices at the expense of our health. This includes those who put their health at risk by engaging in unhealthy lifestyles and self-destructive behavior.

PERSONAL RESPONSIBILITY

In June 2009, ABC News reported on the startling case of Jerri Gray, the mother of Alexander Draper, her 14-year-old handicapped son. This teenager weighed 555 pounds. His morbid obesity put him in the parameter of the triple risk of hypertension, diabetes, and heart troubles. The local South Carolina Department of Social Services believed that Jerri Gray could turn around her son's critical condition by applying some specific treatments. Her failure to follow through with medical appointments triggered some stiff action against her. Her son was placed in foster care. She had to appear in court to face two felony charges, one for custodial interference and a second for child neglect. In this case, outside intervention became necessary. Steps were taken to ensure the enforcement of her duty. It is unfortunate that her son could not realistically take charge of his health because of his age and condition.

As this case demonstrates, the divine promise of a full lifespan collides with the failure of personal responsibility. It is an issue that surfaces in sacred literature. Solomon made it clear that "if you are wise, your wisdom will reward you; if you are a mocker, you alone will suffer."[8] More recently, Josiah Charles Stamp, an economist, stressed the value of personal responsibility: "It is easy to dodge our responsibilities, but we cannot dodge the consequences of dodging our responsibilities."[9]

Many forgo the promise of a full lifespan and fall victim to a premature death. In 2009, the World Health Organization identified the five major causes of premature death: "Childhood nutrition, unsafe sex, alcohol, bad sanitation and hygiene, and high blood pressure are to blame for a quarter of the 60-million premature deaths."

People make poor health choices as they engage in self-destructive behaviors. In 2009, *Newsweek* proclaimed "America's Top Killer: Us." This message was based on Duke University's Ralph Keeney finding claiming, "America's top killer isn't cancer or heart diseases, or even smoking or overeating—it's our inability to make smart choices that lead us to engage in those and other self-destructive behaviors"[10] More than a million people needlessly die due to their own poor decisions. We have the ability to reverse these trends.

STAY IN SHAPE

The offer of a full lifespan is attainable by making the commitment to monitor and adjust one's health. Health is a prerequisite in fulfilling God's mission for our lives. When sickness sidelines us, we can help no one, not even ourselves. The Roman poet Virgil said well that "the greatest wealth is health." Health must be seen as a holistic entity embracing the physical, mental, and spiritual dimensions of life. One must make every effort to nurture life by staying in shape.

PHYSICAL SHAPE

Jim Rohn, motivational speaker and writer, encourages us to take care of our body, for "it's the only place you have to live."[11] Caring for your body is a matter of commitment backed by will power. Practically all the relevant recommendations to be physically healthy can be found on the Internet or at your nearest local library. There is no excuse to fail to use these resources. Your primary care physician is ready to help meet your commitment to sound physical fitness.

Scripture is the surest source of inspiration for life change. In that respect, Jesus stands as the prime example of one who kept his body in great shape. Jesus was filled with energy and vitality as he walked up and down the roads throughout Palestine. Peter said that he "went around doing good and healing all who were under the power of the devil."[12] Of course Jesus did not have any of the conveniences of modern transportation. Neither did he travel by horses, camels, or otherwise. Jesus was a walker. Matthew wrote that Jesus met his first disciples while "walking beside the sea of Galilee."[13] For stress management, walking is perhaps the best and cheapest tool to help us maintain our physical shape. It helps release stress and gives us time to allow the mind to think. We should engage in all physical exercise that will help us develop a healthy and well-balanced body.

MENTAL SHAPE

The United Negro Fund has long had the motto "The mind is a terrible thing to waste." What a great thing it is to come to the realization of the mind's power of handling everything we do.

It is important to monitor our mind. Once the mind fails, there is little left of our personality. It is not simply our cognitive ability; the mind also controls our values and our thoughts. The interrelationship between our physical and mental health is tremendous. Because of this, we have to make a commitment not only to physically walk like Jesus but also to walk with Jesus by embracing his ideal. Paul bids us to have the mind of Christ: "Let this mind be in you that was also in Christ Jesus."[14] By accepting the mind of Christ we can monitor and conquer all the gullibility, brainwashing, and countless pitfalls we face affecting our health.

The power of the mind is increased by our level of maturity. Like fruit growing on a tree, our minds "ripen" as we mature, becoming more effective. A mature mind is a ripening fruit ready to be enjoyed. It allows us to successfully make the many decisions we make each day. Paul describes maturity in these terms: "When I was a child, I talked like a child, I thought like a child, I reasoned like a child. When I became a man, I put childish things behind me."[15] It is most appropriate to maturely monitor and adjust our speech, thought patterns, and reasoning to handle the problems and circumstances at hand.

This mental dimension requires a full emotional balance. We live overloaded lives. We are asked to perform many tasks at home, our workplace and church, and to perform community service. We fall prey to stress. We can learn to cope by adopting readily available stress management techniques.

SPIRITUAL SHAPE

Coordination of the body, mind, and spirit becomes our goal. Spiritual shape is just as important as the others. This takes place when we are able to stay fully charged and to be able to recharge through our practice of spiritual disciplines anchored in prayer and meditation.

Prayer is a source of sanity in our insane world, keeping us in touch with the author of the universe. Most undoubtedly prayer is a most powerful asset in finding a solution to our problems.

It is essential to monitor our prayer life. In our overloaded lives we are asked to perform too many tasks and activities. We are caught up in the rat race for success. We are overwhelmed by the hustle and bustle of modern life. It is good to make room for some form of contemplation away from our busy schedules. The psalmist reminds us that the one who takes time to meditate on God's timeless law is blessed. That person is compared to "a tree planted by the streams of water, which yields fruit in season, and whose leaf does not wither. Whatever he does prospers."[16]

The fruit this tree bears provides us with a robust spiritual life. It yields an unspeakable joy filled with glory and health that modern scientific technology cannot achieve. "A cheerful heart is good medicine, but a crushed spirit dries up the bones"[17] expresses our relief from the stress of life's journey.

HEALTH RESTORATION

Health is a matter of personal responsibility. We must make the commitment to maintain ourselves and, when necessary, restore our health. Fortunately, we have a great health care system at our disposal. Yet Elizabeth McGlynn, associate director of the RAND Health in Santa Barbara, California, suggests, "There is no Perfect Health System," even here in America, the "highest spending-country in health care."[18] One must recall the fierce conflicts stemming from President Barack Obama's attempts to reform America's health care system.

While it is important to turn to your primary care physician, we should also rely on our Great Physician. Jesus gave much of his attention to the ministry of restoration and healing. One-third of his ministry was dedicated to healing the sick. Matthew wrote, "Jesus went throughout Galilee, teaching in their synagogues, preaching the good news of the kingdom, and healing every disease and sickness among the people."[19] The health provision offering protection from "every disease and sickness" is a promise we cannot overlook. Every step should be taken to make this provision a reality.

Restoration is achieved by embracing a new lifestyle. A woman who was caught in the very act of adultery was brought before Jesus to be stoned in accordance with the Jewish law. As the great defender of the weak, Jesus knew better than her accusers. He knew that not one of them could throw the first stone because they had sins of their own. Jesus did not condemn the woman but taught her a valuable lesson that is relevant in the restorative process: "Go now and leave your life of sin."[20] We can surely reverse our self-destructive urges and embrace a healthy lifestyle. It does take courage, but we have the courage to overcome this weakness. We can transform our unhealthy practices into wellness and good health.

Restoration is best achieved with faith. People turn their health around when their faith believes it can be done. There is the story of a woman who suffered for twelve years with a blood problem. Her opportunity came when she heard that Jesus was traveling through her neighborhood. Her faith motivated her to visit Jesus. As it turned out, the crowd was too big for a personal interview. But she endured when she was able to monitor and adjust to the circumstances by just touching the edge of his garment. Her faith paid off. She was fully healed.

MANAGING WITH GRACE

Paul was fully involved with his apostleship when he was struck by an incurable disease. He called it "a thorn in the flesh." While the nature of his affliction was not known, Paul chose to accept it. He was able to rely on the power of God's grace. "My grace is sufficient for you, for my power is made perfect in weakness."[21] Paul was able to adjust to the reality of this affliction for the remainder of his life.

Franklin Delano Roosevelt was similarly afflicted at the height of his political career. He served as a New York state senator, then during the administration of Woodrow Wilson as assistant secretary of the navy. Roosevelt was naturally driven by a lifetime ambition to become president of the United States. In the summer of 1921, Roosevelt was enjoying his vacation at Campobello when he was stricken by poliomyelitis and realized he would never walk again. He had to be carried around or pushed in a wheelchair to get from one place to another. Roosevelt monitored and adjusted to his new condition. His biographer James MacGregor Burns said Roosevelt adjusted well enough to keep the disease from derailing his political career. He went through a physical transformation—"as if compensating for his crippled legs, he developed heavy, muscular shoulders and chest..."[22] Maintaining his sunny disposition, he even managed to make his legs something of a political asset. He gained sympathy with his radiant smiles and his vigorous gestures. Roosevelt managed to become governor of New York and ultimately one of the greatest presidents of the United States.

It is important we learn to manage our "thorn in the flesh" conditions. Leaning on the power of grace, we can make the most of every situation. Health is precious. Yet it can be elusive unless we take the necessary steps to manage it effectively. We must come to the realization there is no perfect health state. Though we may enjoy life for many seasons, the winter of life becomes the most challenging. Paul reflects on that reality when he wrote, "Though outwardly we are wasting away yet inwardly we are being renewed day by day."[23] In this effort, we must sustain ourselves through the divine promise of enjoying good health. Let us nurture the hope and take the steps to make that happen, regardless of the odds.

NOTES

1. Alvin Toffler, *Future Shock* (New York: A Bantam Book, 1970), 2.
2. Roberta Lee, *The Superstress Solution* (New York: Random House, 2010), 7.

3. I Chronicles 4: 10.
4. Proverbs 4:22.
5. Pittsburgh *Post-Gazette,* September 18, 2011, A6.
6. Exodus 23: 26.
7. 3 John 2.
8. Proverbs 9:12.
9. Josiah Charles Stamp, "*Josiah Charles Stamp quotes,*" Thinkexist.com/quotes/josiah_charles_stamp, access 2/11/2013.
10. Ralph Keeney, "'America Top Killer:Us" *Daily Beast,* Orforum.blog.informs.org/files/2009/01/keeney.pdf., access 2/11/2013.
11. Jim Rohn, "Jim Rohn Quotes," *Brainy Quote,* www.sparkpeople.com/mypage_public_journal_individual.asp., access 2/11/2013
12. Acts 9: 38.
13. Matthew 4: 18.
14. Philippians 2:5.
15. I Corinthians 13 : 11.
16. Psalm 1: 3.
17. Proverbs 17:22.
18. Elizabeth A. McGlynn, "Elizabeth McGlynn Publications," *Rand,*www.rand.org/pubs/authors/m/mcglynn_elizabeth_a.html., access 2/11/2013.
19. Matthew 4: 23.
20. John 8: 11.
21. 2 Corinthians 12: 8.
22. James MacGregor Burns, *Roosevelt: The Lion and The Fox* (New York: Harcourt, Brace & World, 1956), 90.
23. I Corinthians 4:16.

Chapter Eight

Managing the Stress of Relational Life

> Bear with each other, and forgive whatever grievances you may have against one another. (Colossians 3:13)

There is a spectacular event that takes place each year in East Africa. I watched a version of it on the CBS news magazine *60 Minutes*. The great migration of wildebeest and zebra from Tanzania to Kenya is the event I mention. This migration involves 1.5 million wildebeests (also called gnus) and 300,000 zebras and their young traveling on an 1,800-mile journey to search for food and water. As we would expect, along the way lie all kinds of dangerous threats as they cross a couple of rivers on their travels from Tanzania north to Kenya. Threats include predators like lions, wild dogs, leopards, and crocodiles that are hungry for these animals.

The meaningful lesson of this great migration is the togetherness that binds the herds. Whether or not they are driven by some instinctual forces, these animals demonstrate a high level of cooperation in action. They are united by a definite common goal in their race to a common destination.

The wildebeest and zebra herds remind us of the bonds linking all of earth's living creatures. As children of the same God, we have at our disposal many tools to manage the stresses of our life in a changing world. This basic principle of harmoniously relating to each other is rooted in God's natural laws. It is a reminder to carry our duty to a higher level, a goal to live in harmonious relationships.

The need for connection, for friendship, was described by New York *Times* columnist David Brooks in his book *The Social Animal*. He underscores that "what drives us ultimately is the need to be understood by others."[1]

THE POLARIZATION OF RELATIONAL LIFE

Unlike the things we have in common with the animal kingdom, we live more than ever in a polarized world. Consider this: The first murder in human history was recorded in the very book of Genesis. Cain murdered his brother Abel. When God confronted him about the whereabouts of his brother, Cain, whose conscience was burdened by this horrific act, reacted coldly: "Am I my brother's keeper?"[2] Or to say it another way, choosing the words of the Roman comic playwright Plautus: "Man is a wolf to man." This maxim stands at the center of Thomas Hobbes' work *Leviathan*, a book of political philosophy that highlights man's instincts towards human destruction.

The twentieth century demonstrated our propensity to destroy one another. In that century we witnessed two major world wars. World War I began with the assassination in Sarajevo of the Austrian prince François-Ferdinand by Serbian terrorists on June 28, 1914. A month later, Austria declared war on Serbia. Major European nations, Russia, Germany, France, England, and, later, the United States declared war against each other. Human ingenuity created all forms of infamous weapons of mass destruction including mustard gas as weapons of war. By the time it was over, eight and half million people had lost their lives.

It was called the "war to end all wars." We all know it wasn't. A few decades following World War I, World War II began in 1939. When Adolph Hitler came to power in Germany, he embarked on a campaign of territorial expansion and conquest. Hitler came to power during a depression where the Weimar Republic tried to pay the war reparations demanded by the World War I ending Treaty of Versailles. The huge debt made the German people suffer more than the rest of us during the Great Depression. Hitler, despite his evil, was seen at the time to be the salvation for a depressed Germany. The governments of England and France only served to encourage his aggression with their policies of appeasement. Hitler invaded several European countries with only mild objections from the other European powers. But when he invaded Poland in September 1939, the allied nations had had enough. England and France declared war on Hitler. The killing continued for six years until 1945 when Germany was defeated in Stalingrad. In Asia, Japan was aligned with Germany to form the axis powers. Japan did its best to destroy China and even invaded U.S. territory at Pearl Harbor to draw the United States into the war. After Germany was destroyed, American President Harry S Truman used nuclear bombs in Nagasaki and Hiroshima to effectively end this war, but at what cost?

The story about Hitler highlights a monstrous crime against humanity. He sought to destroy the Jewish people in Europe, creating extermination camps in his "Final Solution" to what he saw as the Jewish problem. Jews were driven from their homes into concentration camps. Families were not only separated but also destroyed by Hitler's thugs. The Holocaust, the mass destruction of millions of Jews, remains one of the most horrific debacles in human history.

These wars and countless others in the annals of history demonstrate man's inhumanity against man. This inhumanity continues to this day.

UNMANAGED STRESS IN THE FAMILY

It is not just nations where man works to destroy other men. It is also on a personal level. Take a look at Kevin, who fell on hard times during his marriage. He and his estranged wife were unable to fix their broken relationship. They had two children, 8-year-old Madison and 22-month-old Kevin Jr. Kevin's stress made his wife a target. Kevin was unable to handle his fear that his wife would get custody of their children. He was depressed over these thoughts and unable to manage the stress. In the end, Kevin killed his wife and the two children before taking his own life.[3]

Conflicts abound in the family, especially husband and wife. The divorce rate has become catastrophic. Then there are the conflicts between parents and children. We should take the necessary steps to manage these conflicts not only for our survival but for the optimal stability of the family.

INVEST IN RELATIONSHIPS

Our changing world tends to minimize relational interactions. Our technological society ushers in new devices that tend to pull people apart rather than together. Our new interactions are with machines rather than people. We have access today to a number of gadgets such as iPods and iPads, laptops, smart phones, and an array of video games. People have become confined to their own individual world rather than participating in group activities. Gary Small, a psychiatry professor at UCLA, says "The new digital age is altering how we think and interact."[4] These twenty-first-century gadgets lessen the effect of well-established institutions of family life like conversation and meditation.

There is a great need to nurture more personal interrelationships. While our society encourages us in the pursuit of more physical and cognitive environments, the push is not as great when it comes to investing in the relational life. Yet our relationship with others is the only path to fulfillment and satisfaction in life. Dr. Richard Swenson helps us understand the tools of the relational life include "the social (my relationship to others, the emotional (my relationship to myself), and the spiritual, (my relationship to God)."[5] Let us explore how we can best take the necessary steps to nurture and enrich the full scope of our relationships.

OUR RELATIONSHIP TO GOD

Strong healthy relationship begins with a natural connection with God. It is important to know we are talking here about the personal God. Eighteenth-century thinkers, for instance, who were eager to promote the rule of reason, saw the idea of God as a watchmaker. They saw this God as the supreme architect, the designer of the solar system. Sir Isaac Newton, the consummate scientist of the time, conceived of a creator whose existence could not be denied due to the wonders of all creation.

Although we may join them in remembering God as the creator of life and the universe, we must focus here on God as the loving Father who is eager to relate to us in a very personal way. He is the heavenly Father who knows all about us and who cares enough to intervene in every detail of our life. He is the God who has a plan for us. "For I know the plans I have for you, plans to prosper you and not harm you, plans to give you hope and a future."[6] He is the God who helps us handle life's stressful situations.

God's compassionate love as a heavenly Father is illustrated in a story Jesus told of the prodigal son. Here was this young and immature young man whose will led him to venture away from his father. Once he received his share of the inheritance, the son went away to a far country where he squandered everything he had in pursuit of all kinds of pleasures. It reached a low point when he discovered he was broke and hungry and had nothing left. At this stage, he came to his senses and decided to return home. When his father saw him from a distance, the father ran to welcome his return. The happy dad gave his son the warmest of all welcomes. He clothed him, gave him shoes and jewelry, and a special feast where there was much happiness for all.

Investing in our relationship with God is the most manageable stress-busting tool. The beauty is that God truly wants to maintain close ties with every one of us as a loving Father. Even when we venture like straying sheep, he stands ready to warmly welcome us back.

It is imperative we monitor this precious relationship, remembering that God's presence is our warranty against the damage caused by stress. Like the prodigal son, we know it is easy to slide into alienation and isolation. The story of Samson is in this respect even more startling. Here is a prodigal of a different stripe, similar in many ways with the same careless and inconsistent attitude. Endowed with special spiritual power, Samson mismanaged his life to the point of falling into a trap with Delilah. In the end, he became unaware he had lost his strength. Once Delilah cut his hair, the source of his strength, Samson "did not know that the Lord had left him."[7]

Before his death, Samson made some necessary adjustment that allowed him to regain his strength, though he used it as a means of revenge. God is a God of second chance. He leaves the door open to us so we can adjust to his perfect will. Therein ultimately lies our path to an abundant life of peace and fulfillment. Life's best adjustment lies within God's love.

OUR EMOTIONAL RELATIONSHIP

When I was in my early twenties, I experienced the dark side of life. Upon completing my secondary studies at the Lycee Pétion in Port-au-Prince, I thought about becoming a physician as a sure path to a bright future. Unfortunately, I failed the entrance exam. I fell into despair that eventually led to depression.

The turning point took place on March 11, 1966, when I acquired my very first Bible ever. I was directed to the sixth chapter of Matthew's Gospel where Jesus bids us to eliminate worrisome thoughts from our minds. "Do not worry about your life, what you will eat or drink or about your body, what you will wear... do not worry about tomorrow, for tomorrow will worry about itself."[8] As the sun melts away the morning mist these words dispelled my dark shadows. I regained my balance and have been rejoicing ever since.

We are all creatures of our emotions. Our feelings move us up and down depending on the winds of the day. When he learned about the death of his son Absalom, David's heart dived in deep sorrow. Consider that at the time Absalom was at war with David. When he learned the news, David was shaken and wept over Absalom. We encounter the same David in brighter days when, bubbling with joy, he exclaimed, "This is the day that the Lord has made, let us rejoice and be glad in it."[9] It is thus important to attain a level of stability.

EMOTIONAL STABILITY

Depression and stressed feelings generally come from some emotional disorder. The equilibrium of our life hangs on our emotions. Since our emotional life is of such utmost importance, it needs then to be monitored to attain and maintain our stability. Psychologists classify emotions into two basic categories, calling them pleasant and unpleasant. They are also described as positive or negative. While twelve emotions are mentioned in philosophical literature, nine are considered unpleasant: fear, anger, jealousy, shame, sorrow, and so on. The other three are pleasant emotions: love, joy, and awe. We should make sure our positive emotions, though minority in number, become the majority of our thinking for our own well-being.

In the homes of people living in cold winter, there is usually a thermostat set at a definite degree to keep the heat at a comfortable level. We all have an inner thermostat we need to set when it comes to our emotional relationships. I suggest that we set it on the level of rejoicing. Paul made the call for us when he wrote, "Rejoice in the Lord always, and again I say rejoice."[10] He is referring here to a spiritual joy that defies all outer weather and life circumstances. We can only enjoy that level of spiritual joy when we have the conviction of the sovereignty of God in our lives and all the events connected with us.

EMOTIONAL SECURITY

It all boils down to developing a clear awareness of an emotional security that is anchored with God. This security comes from a conviction that God's love comes to us from our heavenly Father. "We are God's workmanship created in Christ's image to do good works which God prepared in advance for us to do."[11] We have God's guarantee of life within the bounds of his unfailing love to remove all the negative feelings of loneliness and isolation.

Because of his love for us, our emotional security is reinforced further by the conviction that God has our back, to use the military expression. We rely on our heavenly Father because He cares and knows what is best for us. "I am the Lord your God, who teaches you what is best for you, who directs you in the way you should go."[12] Such an assurance builds in us an emotional security that assuages our deepest fears.

SOCIAL RELATIONSHIP

The conclusion of Paul's letters describes the reality of the relational life. The apostle takes the time to send greetings and express his affection for friends and acquaintances of the faith. The end of his letter to the Romans is a particular hallmark. A long list of names mentions those fellow workers who risked their lives for him, especially Priscilla and Aquila. He recalled Epenetus as a dear friend and Rufus' mother who was his mother. He concluded with this call to the entire church: "Greet one another with a holy kiss."[13] The message is clear: we are created to work on our relationships. We are connected with each other. We are not islands unto ourselves. Our challenge then is to make every effort to maintain the links that bind us to one another.

Paul's tone of affection reminds us we are created for relationship. No fulfillment is possible without each other. Abraham Maslow's hierarchy of needs reminds us that we are all connected. The evidence is overwhelming when we consider the first five physiological needs in the hierarchy: for safety, love and belongingness, self-esteem, and self-fulfillment. Each one is met by our relationship with one another. We should therefore take all steps necessary to create and maintain our harmonious relationships.

RISING ABOVE INTERPERSONAL CONFLICT

Genesis features an emotional reunion between brothers long separated by conflicts. Joseph endured the hatred of his brothers caused by their jealous spirit of his glorious dreams. That hatred led them to commit despicable acts against Joseph: they left him for dead in an empty well, and they sold him to Ishmaelite traders. The brothers were separated for a long time. But when Joseph ascended the Egyptian throne, he rose above these conflicts. He sent for them, and when they had gathered under one roof, Joseph "kissed all his brothers and wept over them."[14] He took the huge step here to overcome his animosity. It takes courage to put aside an unpleasant past and start over in peace. It also takes some specific skills.

INTERPERSONAL SKILL

The Corsini *Dictionary of Psychology* defines Interpersonal skill as the aptitude to maintain "effective relationships with others, such as cooperating, communicating thought and feeling, assuming appropriate social responsibilities and exhibiting adequate flexibility."

That gives us the challenge to develop and maintain harmonious relations. Reaching such a noble objective requires the consistent application of effective skills.

The ability of monitoring and making the right adjustment for healthy relationships is equal to the ability to be flexible.

It is undeniable that the correct adjustment is connected with our ability to forgive. Joseph reconciled with his brothers when he freed himself from his resentment and forgave his brothers for their past transgressions.

FORGIVENESS

Forgiveness holds healing both for ourselves and our relationship to others. McCullough, Sandage, and Worthington examined forgiveness from a psychological point of view and arrived at the conclusion you can "improve your physical, mental and spiritual relationships by maintaining a forgiving lifestyle."[15]

Jesus suggested we cultivate forgiveness as a lifestyle. Peter once asked Jesus about the practice of forgiveness. "Lord, how many times shall I forgive my brother when he sins against me? Up to seven times? Jesus answered, I tell you, not seven times but seventy times-seven."[16] Forgiveness is ongoing. It is the loving tool at our disposal to free our minds and souls from bitterness and hostility.

RADIANT LIVES

Our interpersonal skill cultivating healthy relationships is reinforced by the emotion of joy. As we monitor the emotions of life, we can function more effectively and lead radiant lives: "Those who look to him are radiant."[17] We realize the dividends we reap with our joy. We stand ready to reap the benefits of a radiant life. Joy becomes an important ingredient in enhancing and strengthening our relationships.

The *British Medical Journal* published a study in 2008 that "finds joy to be contagious." Happiness is not an individual but a collective phenomenon. It spreads from one person to the next. People with radiant lives are like magnets pulling others toward their circles.

NOTES

1. David Brooks, "David Brooks Wants to be Friends," *Bing* www.thedailybeast.com/newsweek/2011/02/27/david-brooks. Access 2/11/2013
2. Genesis 4:9.
3. Story reported in the Pittsburgh *Post-Gazette*, September 25, 2013.

4. Gary Small, "Brains on Overdrive," *Psychology Today*, www.psychologytoday.com/blog/brain-bootcamp/200906/is.,access 2/11/2013.

5. Swenson, *Margin*, 35.

6. Jeremiah 29:11.

7. Judges 16:20.

8. Matthew 6:25, 34.

9. Psalm 118:24.

10. Philippians 4: 4.

11. Ephesians 2: 20.

12. Isaiah 48:17.

13. Romans 16:16.

14. Genesis 45:15.

15. Michael E. McCullough, Stephen J. Sandage, and Everett L. Worthington, Jr, *To Forgive Is Human*, (Downers Grove, Ill.: InterVarsity Press, 1997), 18.

16. Matthew 18: 21-22.

17. Psalm 34: 5.

Chapter Nine

Embracing Change

> His compassions never fail, they are new every morning. (Lamentations 3:23-24)

September 11, 2001, began normally enough. People around the country came and went about their daily routine: going to work; going to school; catching buses, trains, and planes; watching TV; making and reporting to appointments; and so forth and so on. This routine forever changed when nineteen hijackers boarded two American Airlines and two United Airlines planes in Boston, Washington, and Newark International Airport. At 8:46 that day, American Airlines flight 11 hit the north tower of New York's World Trade Center. The south tower was next. It was struck by United Airlines Flight 175. The Pentagon was hit later by American Airlines Flight 77. The fourth plane, United Airlines Flight 93, bound for the White House, crashed in Shanksville, Pennsylvania, when passengers took matters into their own hands and prevented another attack.

The events of September 11 drastically altered history. They provoked a tremendous shift toward monitoring and adjusting our lives to the consequences of this terrorist attack. The United States government took drastic action to protect American security. Nearly overnight the airport security instituted severe measures including ID checks, luggage searches, and intrusive pat downs. President George Bush helped create a Department of Homeland Security aimed at strengthening America's security. A united country embraced these new changes so we could lead a normal life free from the threat of terrorism.

NEW PERSPECTIVE

We have developed a new perspective on life as we seek to cope with this stress of change. This new perspective allows us to reevaluate our values so we might focus on what is truly important. The tragic events of the magnitude of September 11 remind us not only of the value of life but also its fragility. It is important for us to engage in a continual renewal of our minds: "Do not conform any longer to the pattern of this world, but be transformed by the renewing of the mind."[1]

A new perspective helps us accept new ways to solving problems. Naaman was cured of a debilitating disease only when he embraced a new perspective. As commander of the army of King Ben-Hadad of Syria, he was a famous military strategist. He was also afflicted with leprosy, back then a hopeless and helpless disease. A servant girl working in Naaman's home suggested a relevant solution to help his master. Familiar with the renowned miracle-worker Elisha, the girl recommended her master seek his help.

When the news reached King Ben-Hadad, he received it in a positive way. The king, though, sought to handle things according to established protocol. He wrote a letter to the king of Israel asking for his help. Naaman then traveled from Syria to Israel. When the letter was delivered, the king of Israel was puzzled, not knowing what to do. Elisha brought relief to the king's uncertainty and a solution to Naaman's affliction.

THINKING OUTSIDE THE BOX

Like Ben-Hadad, Naaman was thinking inside the box. In line with his custom, he expected to be received by Elisha and go through some kind of rituals. So when the prophet sent him the simple suggestion to dip himself seven times in the Jordan River to cleanse and restore his flesh, he was not at all amused. His servants needed to convince him to think outside the box: "My father, if the prophet had told you to do some great thing, would you not have done it? How much more, then, when he tells you, 'Wash and be cleansed.'"[2] When he obeyed the prophet by washing in the Jordan, he was cured. His flesh was restored and the effects of the disease were no longer present.

We cannot escape the reality of change. An appropriate response to a new situation begins when we have an open-minded attitude and accept the reality that things are changing. You cannot use the benefits of the new opportunities if you remain in the past and continue to adopt worn-out ideas. The catchphrase "thinking outside the box" can be relevant to our renewal thought process. It implies a new approach to the way we look at problems and to accept change. It is a relevant tool that helps us embrace the changes taking place every day. Naaman received his healing blessing only when he agreed to try a new approach without knowing the results. Fortunately he got a favorable result.

MONITOR AND ADJUST TO PHYSICAL CHANGES

My father is now ninety-four years old. It is quite a feat to reach this age anywhere, but more so in Haiti, where life expectancy hovers around fifty years. I count it a blessing to still be able to enjoy his presence with us. I seize on every opportunity to call him and enjoy hearing the sound of his voice. It crosses my mind sometimes that the boundaries between time and eternity are blurred.

What also strikes me is the huge difference between the father I knew when I was young and the father I now have. Once a strong and vigorous man, he was a farmer in mountainous Haiti where he walked long distances, climbed hills, carried heavy loads, and met every challenge to provide for his family of ten. The father I have now is no longer an active individual. I watch with amazement as he sits in a rocking chair napping and rocking as the day moves on.

I think about the impact time makes on our bodies. With the right attitude, we can develop the ability to effectively handle the many changes in our personal lives. The apostle Paul was conscious of that very issue when he wrote: "Therefore we do not lose heart. Though outwardly we are wasting away, yet inwardly we are being renewed day by day."[3] Such an attitude calls us to be realistic about our condition. We should learn to accept the conditions coming our way as we move through the seasons of our lives.

MONITOR AND ADJUST TO NATURAL CHANGES

In a special report on recent natural disasters, *Time* magazine editors looked at the topic of the earth's restlessness. The editors suggested, "Our planet is unsettled, unruly, a work in progress....When tectonic plates move and an earthquake occurs...millions of human lives can be profoundly altered within hours and days."[4] These days, we witness this alteration more and more. An earthquake in Haiti killed an estimated 300,000 souls while leaving another million homeless. Another earthquake in Japan killed some 25,000. The tsunami that followed seemed almost surreal, like a disaster movie, as we watched houses and cars carried away like toys. There were tornadoes in

Tuscaloosa, Alabama, and Joplin, Missouri, and more indescribable destruction. Disasters large and small are ongoing around us. Survivors see their lives change overnight in ways that surpass their understanding. In each one of these situations, it helps to be well equipped with the ability to cope.

EXPECT THE BEST

One of our greatest desires is to control our destiny. It would be reassuring to know our future and be able to master the details of our life's journey. That is the main reason why as rational beings we insist on planning and setting goals. We plan, yet we cannot have the least inkling of what will happen tomorrow.

Yet despite all the uncertainties of life, one must always be aware of the unexpected. This option is only possible when we keep hope alive.

The invalid man by the pool of Bethesda teaches us this very lesson. He was crippled for some thirty-eight years. His hope of a brighter day remained with the regular appearance of an angel that would stir the water of a pool. The hitch, however, was that only the first one to reach the troubled water was healed. Having lost his limbs, he was always at a disadvantage. He must have nurtured the conviction of expecting the best since he refused to give up. He continued to show up every morning at the pool. His faith was rewarded when Jesus showed up to heal him. It was an unexpected event. Jesus bypassed the daily routine by ordering the man to "Get up! Pick up your mat and walk."[5]

PREPARE FOR THE WORST

On January 28, 1986, people awoke looking forward to the excitement of the space shuttle Challenger's flight with Christa McAuliffe on board. From Concord, New Hampshire, she was the teacher selected from more than eleven thousand applicants to be the first ordinary citizen for the Teacher in Space project. As an educator, I was also excited over the prospect of following her acts in space. Classrooms tuned in to watch the launch. Then, the unexpected happened. At 11:38 a.m. EST, the spaceship broke apart just 73 seconds into flight off the coast of Florida. Christa McAuliffe and her six fellow astronauts perished in this accident.

I am by no means a person who dabbles in pessimism; I have chosen to anchor my life wholeheartedly with a bedrock faith that God watches over us and that everything will be all right. This is by the way a song I inherited from my Haitian religious culture: "Thank you, Jesus, everything is going to be all right." This song helped me withstand many of life's toughest storms.

In spite of my sunny disposition, I find it important to make room for the unforeseen. That belief can handle either the thrill of victory or the agony of defeat. We have to make room for what is known as Murphy's Law, that is, "Anything that can go wrong will go wrong." That is the reason why in the best of the possible worlds, I still expect the best while being prepared for the worst. It is hard to determine how many people prepared themselves for the Challenger disaster that has marked our national consciousness. Yet it is wise to seek the reliable power to withstand whatever may come our way.

RESILIENCY

We must be able to rise above stressful situations and adverse circumstances. We need to be resilient. The source of this resiliency comes from our ability to find meaning in life, an issue that is closely connected with the quest for life's purpose. Viktor Frankl reminds us: "Those who have a 'why' to live, can bear with almost any 'how.'"[6] Purpose is the natural step available to us as we cope with the change of stress.

Helen Keller gives us quite an inspiring example. She lived a meaningful life despite the obstacles that filled every step of her difficult journey. At the age of nineteen months she contracted scarlet fever or meningitis that left her both deaf and blind. She managed to somehow enjoy an extraordinary life. Anne Sullivan helped her blossom as she learned to communicate and relate to the outside world. Helen became the first deaf and blind person to earn a Bachelor of Arts degree. Helen lived a full life as author, political activist, and lecturer. She knew she was living in the world for a purpose. As she expressed it, "Sick or well, blind or seeing, bond or free, we are here for a purpose, and however we are situated, we please God better with useful deeds than with many prayers of pious resignation."[7]

A purpose for living is the engine that drives people to action. We can become so energized that no mountain is too high to conquer. Paul was similarly driven for action. He discovered that his life mission was to be a servant of Christ's grace and to "preach to the Gentiles the unsearchable riches of Christ."[8] No power on earth could deter him from this noble mission. Still, he endured a long list of hardships to fulfill his mission: "I have been constantly on the move. I have been in danger from rivers, in danger from bandits, in danger from my own countrymen, in danger from Gentiles; in danger in the city, in danger in the country, in danger at sea; and in danger from false brothers. I have labored and toiled and have often gone without sleep. I have known hunger and thirst and often gone without food. I have been cold and naked."[9]

There is a definite price connected with carrying out one's life purpose. It takes determination to keep one's eyes on the prize. To effectively make it, we need to apply Paul's recommendation in his letter to the Hebrews. "Let us fix our eyes on Jesus, the author and perfecter of our faith, who for the joy set before him endured the cross, scorning its shame and sat down at the right hand of the throne of God."[10]

CONFIDENCE IN GOD

If we were to exclusively dwell on the countless tragedies that could affect us, life becomes an impossible venture. Fortunately, we have a positive option by relying on the mind of Christ when it comes to dealing with life's uncertainties. Jesus teaches us: "Do not worry about tomorrow, for tomorrow will take care of itself. Each day has enough trouble of its own."[11] This statement keeps us from descending into the pit of anxiety and worry. As we continue through life, our confidence in God helps us rise above all our fears, the things that would otherwise paralyze our lives.

Ena Zizi's story inspires our confidence in God. This sixty-nine-year-old lady had gone to Haiti's National Cathedral to pray when the epic quake struck Port-au-Prince, on January 12, 2010. The cathedral collapsed, leaving Ena under the rubble where she remained for seven long days. She had spoken with a vicar for a few days before he became silent. When she was miraculously pulled from the rubble by a Mexican rescue team, she was covered with dust and severely dehydrated. She confessed that prayer helped her survive the ordeal: "I talked to my boss, God. And I didn't need any more humans." Her story is a modern-day illustration of David's confidence in God: "Even though I walk through the valley of the shadow of death, I fear no evil, for you are with me."[12] It is reassuring that we daily walk in God's presence.

POSITIVE CHANGE

A few months after the earthquake, I and a team of American volunteers were in Haiti looking for ways and means to bring relief. We were also looking for an effective strategy to become active in the reconstruction of this devastated country. We were returning to our vehicle when a team member excitedly broke the news of financial assistance. Her organization had received a substantial matching grant to allow the building of a technical school that would train workers for the reconstruction of Haiti. She read the news from an e-mail received on her mobile phone. We rejoiced over this great news helping to fulfill our deepest desires to help such a great cause.

Monitoring and adjusting to technological changes is a positive response to reality. Although technology has its adverse effects, one cannot ignore how it can help improve our living condition. Technology improvements remain the major change that has taken place over the past two centuries. As an example, communication has connected people throughout the world. The Haitian mountains were an unlikely place to receive instant messages, but improvements in technology have made instant messaging a reality, making us more accessible to one another. It becomes easier to quickly communicate with people in other countries and continents.

Keeping up with the latest technological development can be mind boggling. Portable devices such as laptops and mobile phones continue to evolve and improve every day. Consider this latest technology: the tablet, a device that can access video, music, and e-books. Though it is a tremendous challenge to keep up with the daily developments taking place, we run the risk of being left behind if we do not find a way to use these advances.

CHANGE AGENTS

We have been engaged in looking into the events that have the greatest impact on the course of our lives. Such a strategy implies a passive attitude. But a proactive attitude can give us a better option to drive change. It is possible to not just be subject to change but also to take control of what our lives ought to be, coordinated with God's plan. God gives us the power of choice to effectively handle life's threatening circumstances.

Robert Downs' *Books That Changed the World* is a review of the great works that revolutionized our ideas about the universe and ourselves. His book describes a gallery of just twenty-seven thinkers, scientists, and religious leaders who made significant contributions in changing the world. At the top of the list is the Bible, the book of books whose influence is greater than the rest. The Bible contains the word of God that is available to us to effectively navigate life's many problems. After the Bible comes Homer's *Iliad* and *The Odyssey,* two of the greatest masterpieces that helped shape Western civilization.

Downs ends his list with what would appear to be a rather ordinary figure that made an extraordinary impact on our world: Rachel Carson, the author of *Silent Spring.* Carson was born and raised in Springdale, Pennsylvania. She was an eminent marine biologist who focused on "the overwhelming problem of pollution of the air, water, and land which was increasingly disturbing the conscience of the American people."[13] Her work opened the eyes of her generation who were being poisoned by our daily exposure to pesticides. Her legacy inspired others to protect the living world and its creatures. Her book ultimately led to the creation of the Environmental Protection Agency.

All of us have the potential to become agents of change. God created us with the unique ability to see the world in a fresh way. Men and women received from God the stewardship of nature.

We also have the opportunity to conquer stress by serving others. Instead of focusing on our own overwhelming issues, we can invest all our resources into the lives of others. It is a paradox that has proved itself throughout time. Solomon offered this example: "A generous man will prosper. He who refreshes others will himself be refreshed."[14] Marcus Aurelius, the Roman emperor and philosopher, saw the meaning of life in the form of mutual support. "Human beings," he wrote, were made to help others."[15] We can become instruments engaged in changing lives. There is no greater or nobler task.

NOTES

1. Romans 12:2.
2. 2 Kings 5:13.
3. 2 Corinthians 4:10.
4. "Japan: Out of the Shadows," *Time,* www.time.com/time/magazine/article/0,9171,924154.00.html., access 2/11/2013.
5. John 5:8.
6. Victor Frankl, "Viktor Frankl Quotes," *Bing,*Thinkexist.com/quotation/those_who_have_a-why-to_live.
7. Hellen Keller, "Search Quotes," *Gaiam Life,* Blog.gaiam.com/quotes/authors.helen-keller?page=4., access 2/11/2013.
8. Ephesians 3: 8.
9. 2 Corinthians 11: 26-27.
10. Hebrews 12: 2.
11. Matthew 6:34.
12. Psalm 23:4.
13. Robert Downs, *Books That Changed the World* (New York: A Mentor Book, 1983), 329.
14. Proverbs 11:25.
15. Marcus Aurelius, "The case for an Optimistic Stoicism, *The Daily Beast "*www.thedailybeast.com/newsweek/2010/01/01/the-case-for.

Epilogue

Life is a challenging journey filled with uncertainty, unpredictability, and many uncontrollable events. To reach our destination, our journey is like a car traveling on a road filled with bumps. Detour signs are posted here and there to reroute us from our carefully mapped plan. The same is true in other modes of transportation. When compared with an airplane flight, turbulence is expected and the flight attendants take time to prepare passengers for possible emergencies. When traveling by sea, the winds and the waves are factored into our plans as we prepare the course of the journey. Before boarding the ship, people are drilled with floating devices in case of emergency.

Just as we prepare ourselves for travel, we must also be prepared to cope with the stresses created by the bumps and turbulence and wind changes in our lives. A planned strategy of monitoring and adjusting to expect these changes is appropriate. It keeps us from being frustrated and depressed. When we learn to accept that we do not know what might happen from one day to the next, we have learned how to cope.

Consider the case of Zachariah, the father of John the Baptist. According to tradition, this priest went to the temple to offer a sacrifice. There Zachariah met with an angel who revealed the coming birth of a son. Zachariah could hardly believe this prophecy when he considered not only his own advanced age but also the age of his wife Elizabeth. When he doubted this prophecy, the angel rebuked him by silencing him until the child's birth. When he finally came out of the temple, Zechariah needed to monitor and adjust. This articulate, now silenced, man was able to communicate only through sign language for the duration of his wife's pregnancy.

So was it with Ludwig von Beethoven. At the height of his productive life as a music composer, he became deaf and could no longer hear the wonders of his creations. Because of his deafness he became a hermit, isolating himself from society. He needed to monitor and adjust to communicate with family and friends. Around 1818, when his communication difficulties became unbearable, Beethoven carried paper with him so people could write what they wanted to tell him or ask him. Those became known as the "Conversation Books."

It must have been difficult for both of them to accept their new condition. Consider what Oliver Wendell Holmes said when it comes to life-changing events: "To reach the port of heaven, we have to sail with the wind and sometimes against it—but we cannot drift, nor lie at anchor."[1]

Change comes in countless forms. Despite the pain and frustration that the innovations of technology bring, when we monitor and adjust, we can cope with the reality of change. To monitor and adjust actually requires a life-long commitment to our own personal development. Some years ago, Congress adopted legislation called "No Child Left Behind" whose goal was to make sure all children master basic educational standards. We cannot afford being left behind in any area. Commitment to long-life learning is a sure strategy to help us develop.

Change invades all our plans and works. Those people who are forced to change careers several times have learned to adjust to the evolving needs of the job market.

Our bodies also change daily. This particular change confronts us with the greatest challenges, especially as our health deteriorates due to aging.

Whatever changes in our lives, we need to rely on everlasting values to carry us through our troubles. These values include faith, hope, and love. They are the three cornerstones of daily victorious living.

In the end, we should be ready for the ultimate change as we prepare for our end of time. Paul prepares our minds for this event: "I tell you a mystery: We will not all sleep, but we will all be changed –in a flash, in the twinkling of an eye, at the last trumpet…for the perishable must clothe itself with imperishable, and the mortal with immortality."[2]

Through it all, let us move with the conviction that we can endure. The many changes of life can only reinforce our faith in God who controls all living things. Relying on his everlasting arms, we will enjoy an abundant life.

NOTES

1. Oliver Wendell Holmes, "Oliver Wendell Holmes Quotes," Thinexist.com/quotation/to _reach_a_port_we_must-sail, access 2/12/2013.

2. I Corinthians 15:51&53

Bibliography

Beecher Harriet Stowe. *Uncle Tom's Cabin*. New York: Barnes and Noble Classics, 2003.
Corsini, Raymond. *Dictionary of Psychology*. Ann Arbor, Mich.: Braun-Brumfield, 1999.
Downs, Robert. *Books That Changed the World*. New York: A Mentor Book, 1983
Eiseley, Loren. *The Unexpected Universe*. San Diego: A Harvest/HBJ Book, 1969.
Gombrich, E. H. *A Little History of the World*. New Haven and London: Yale University Press, 1985
Kegan, Jerome and Ernest Havemann..*Psychology: An Introduction*. Harcourt Brace, 1972.
King, Martin Luther Jr.. *Strength To Love*. New York: Pocket Books, 1968.
Lee, Roberta. *Superstress Solution*. New York: Random House, 2010
McCullough, Micahel E. and Stephen J. Sandage, and Everett L. Worthington, Jr. *To Forgive Is Human*. Downers Grove, Ill.: InterVarsity Press, 1997.
Obama, Barack, *Dreams from My Father*. New York: Three Rivers Press, 1995.
Pamphile, Leon D. The Mind of Christ:Your Weapon of Victory. Nashville: American Christian Writers, 2005.
Swenson, Richard A., M.D. *Margin: Restoring Emotional, Physical, Financial and Time Reserves to Overloaded Lives*. Colorado Springs, Colo.: Navpress, 1992.
Toffler, Alvin. *Future Shock*. New York: A Bantam Book, 1970.
Wells Albert. M, Jr., *Inspiring Quotations*. Nashville: Thomas Nelson Publishers, 1988, 90.
Toffler, Alvin. *Future Shock*. New York: A Bantam Book, 1970.
Wells Albert. M, Jr., *Inspiring Quotations*. Nashville: Thomas Nelson Publishers, 1988, 90.

www.ingramcontent.com/pod-product-compliance
Lightning Source LLC
Chambersburg PA
CBHW070645300426
44111CB00013B/2274